Words

The Bible Day by Day
September–December 2010

HODDER &
STOUGHTON

First published in Great Britain in 2010 by Hodder & Stoughton
an Hachette UK company

1

A CIP catalogue record for this title is available from the British Library

ISBN 978 0 340 99542 6

Typeset in Minion by Avon DataSet Ltd, Bidford on Avon, Warwickshire

Printed and bound in Great Britain
by Clays Ltd, St Ives plc

Hodder & Stoughton policy is to use papers that are natural, renewable
and recyclable products and made from wood grown in sustainable forests.
The logging and manufacturing processes are expected to conform to the
environmental regulations of the country of origin.

Hodder & Stoughton Ltd
338 Euston Road
London NW1 3BH

www.hodderfaith.com

Contents

Sundays

Psalm 119, the longest in the Psalter, repeatedly
affirms that God's revealed word is sure, pure and
endures.

From the writer of *Words of Life*

We don't have to be lost in a maze to be puzzled; life offers plenty of questions. Questions thread through the chapters we consider in Mark's Gospel; likewise in the portions of 1 Corinthians. Our guest writer, Major Max Sturge, poses questions in his study of Exodus. The second half of Genesis focuses on Jacob's maze-like sojourn – how can his detours come out right?

When we reflect on suffering, whether ours or others', questions naturally arise. While we can't see the end result, we wonder. We feel as if we're living in a spiritual photographic darkroom, but realise it's the only place the final picture can be fully developed. Bible commentator Adam Clarke reminds us: 'Affliction sanctified is a great blessing; unsanctified, it is an additional curse.'

In Advent we ask with others, 'What Child is this?' Key players leading up to the birth of Christ have particular questions. And the questions don't end with Christmas: Mary and Joseph's questions continue throughout Jesus' childhood; at age twelve, Jesus seems quite at home in the midst of questions in the temple. The final day of the year rounds out our questions with the definitive answer – 'Trust'.

On Sundays we continue to consider eight-verse sections of Psalm 119 and find questions sprinkled throughout. Nevertheless, the acrostic psalm refers us to God's Word in all but one of its 176 verses and appeals for a wholehearted love for God's Word and way. We join the psalmist and pray: 'Let me live whole and holy, soul and body, so I can always walk with my head held high' (Psalm 119:80, *MSG*).

Evelyn Merriam
New York, USA

Abbreviations

AB   *Amplified Bible* © 1965 Zondervan.

CEV   *Contemporary English Version* © 1995 American Bible Society, NY, USA.

JBP   *The New Testament in Modern English* © J. B. Phillips, Geoffrey Bles, 1958, 1959, 1960, 1972 HarperCollins Publishers.

JMT   *James Moffatt Translation* © 1922, 1924, 1925, 1926, 1935. HarperCollins Publishers.

MSG   *The Message,* Eugene H. Peterson © 1993, 1994, 1995, 1996, 2000, 2001, 2002. Used by permission of NavPress Publishing Group.

NASB   *New American Standard Bible* © 1960, 1962, 1963, 1968, 1971, 1972, 1973, 1975, 1977, 1995 by The Lockman Foundation. Used by permission.

NEB   *New English Bible* © 1961, 1970 Oxford University Press.

NETS   *New English Translation of the Septuagint* © 2000 by the International Organisation for Septuagint and Cognate Studies, Inc. Used by permission of Oxford University Press.

NKJV   *New King James Bible* © 1982 by Thomas Nelson, Inc. Used by permission. All rights reserved.

NLT   *New Living Translation* © 1996, 1998, Tyndale House Publishers.

NRSV   *New Revised Standard Version Bible: Anglicised Edition* © 1989, 1995 Division of Christian Education of the National Council of the Churches of Christ in the USA. Used by permission. All rights reserved.

SASB   *The Song Book of The Salvation Army* © 1986 The General of The Salvation Army.

WNT   *New Testament in Modern Speech,* Richard Francis Weymouth © 1978 Kregle Publications, Grand Rapids, Michigan, USA.

YLT   *Young's Literal Translation,* Robert Young (1898), reprinted by Baker Book House, Grand Rapids, Michigan, USA.

Questions Escalate
Mark 11–13

Introduction

We continue with Mark's account of the life of Christ. The chapters we consider take place in and around Jerusalem. We listen in as people with various motivations bombard Jesus with questions.

He uses one question's unlikely topic, a widow, as a springboard for teaching about eternal life, for warning about victimising others and for commending sincere, sacrificial giving.

Jesus is just days away from the cross, yet he patiently gives thoughtful replies to all questioners and goes on to clear up some commonly held muddled ideas.

Questions can help us to learn and grow. A well-known leadership expert asked a gathering of Christians at the United Nations to consider what questions they were willing to ask themselves. For example:

- Am I visibly honouring Christ in my life and is he pleased with me?
- Am I attentive to others for their sakes?
- Are people better off because I've been with them?

Jesus poses some questions of his own in these chapters. Perhaps through them the Living Word will prompt some questions in our lives as well.

On the Fringe

*'Go into the village ahead of you, and immediately as you enter it,
you will find tied there a colt that has never been ridden;
untie it and bring it' (v. 2, NRSV).*

The detail Mark uses suggests an eyewitness account, so perhaps Peter, Mark's source, was one of those sent for the donkey in Bethphage. In verses 2 and 3 Mark uses his signature adverb, *euthys* (immediately). Jesus says that the animal will be returned straightway after use. He also says the disciples will find the colt immediately on entering the village, at the edge of town.

Who would have thought that a dwelling on the outskirts would be the place to provide the necessary donkey for the prophesied procession of the Messiah into Jerusalem?

In some parts of the world the most desired and costly property is closest to the city centre where the activity of commerce and government transpires. Less desirable areas on the fringe are left to those with little means and often little hope of change. In certain areas of South America's Andes mountains those with less means live in the heights since the property at the lowest, most accessible elevation is most desirable.

But it isn't just those without money who live on the fringes of life. Within any social group there are people on the fringe, not part of the 'in' crowd for whatever reason. Jesus not only noticed but drew in people the society of his day dismissed or thought useless. In its finest moments the body of Christ continues to be aware of those who are overlooked and need assistance or an advocate.

In a sense, aren't we all at the edge of the village, the edge of the crowd, on the fringe? At least, we feel that we are at times. Yet Jesus sees us as individuals, values us and gives us opportunities to contribute. Who better to reach out to others at the edge than those who have been drawn in by God's love?

We note that it was obedient disciples who carried out Christ's direction to go to the edge of town on what must have seemed an unusual task, yet one vital to his mission. Our obedience to the Lord may involve some unusual tasks that are still vital.

A House of Prayer

'He was teaching and saying, "Is it not written, 'My house shall be called a house of prayer for all the nations?' " ' (v. 17, NRSV).

My husband and I had never visited Europe before, so noticed some things we weren't accustomed to seeing. Centuries-old towns were often built around a large church at their centre. We realised that church attendance had been waning and didn't expect that we would be among more than a handful at prayers in a small side chapel in one town. What did surprise us was a civic arts festival set up in part of the nave and the many stalls clustered around the outside of the church like toadstools near the base of an old tree.

When Jesus leaves the crowds of palm-waving well-wishers in Jerusalem and enters the temple, he simply assesses the situation and leaves for Bethany to spend the night (v. 11). The next day he would return with a goal.

Recently the high priest had authorised a temple market to sell approved items needed for sacrifices. Additionally, for a small fee, Greek and Roman coins in common circulation could be exchanged for the required image-free Jewish coins required for payment of the annual temple tax. Greed inflated prices then as now.

The temple merchants Jesus encounters are not in the holy of holies, the court of the priests, or the court of Israel – places of worship for Jewish men or women – but on the fringe in the court of the Gentiles. The court of the Gentiles was not only host to temple commerce, but it had become a shortcut for people carrying general merchandise from one part of Jerusalem to another.

The church we visited was the community's centre, but less for worship than for entertainment, buying and selling. Jesus sees that the temple's purpose as a place of prayer has been hijacked by an organised band of greedy merchants who are especially disrespectful to the outsiders – the non-Jews. He takes action for the Gentiles and for God's purposes.

To ponder:

The gospel's all-encompassing offer of salvation is meant for whoever comes to God through Christ. How do we enable that mission to continue unhindered?

Question of Authority

'But I have a testimony greater than John's. The works that the Father has given me to complete, the very works that I am doing, testify on my behalf that the Father has sent me. And the Father who sent me has himself testified on my behalf' (John 5:36, 37, NRSV).

In the temple the previous day, Jesus quoted an Old Testament prophet when he said that God's house should be a place of prayer (see Isaiah 56:7). Although Jesus' teaching about the temple astounds and encourages the common people, it threatens those whose corruption enables the travesties. The religious leaders plan to kill him (v. 18).

After a night in Bethany, Jesus and the disciples return to Jerusalem. Jesus doesn't avoid the temple, but walks through its courts as if inviting the scrutiny of the leaders. Representatives sent by the assembly of experts in Jewish law confront Jesus with questions about what he said and did in the temple the previous day and about his ministry, which kept gaining popular acclaim: What is the nature of your authority? Who gave you such authority?

In typical rabbinical repartee, Jesus counters that he will answer if they answer his question first: was John the Baptist's ministry of human or divine origin? It is a no-win situation for the leaders. If they admit it was God-given, he could ask why they hadn't believed John and the one to whom John pointed. If they say that John's ministry was humanly inspired, they would probably enrage the crowd, possibly to riot, especially since John had recently been martyred for his faith.

So the learned leaders feebly say they don't know. They refuse to face the truth. Unbelief blinds. Since they don't give a firm answer, in effect they reject John and Jesus as messengers of God. They neither defend their position nor admit they are wrong. They are not unlike public figures of our day.

———

To ponder:

Is the Lord asking us to declare ourselves for him in some particular way? If we ask him, he will help us to be forthright and faithful under his authority.

Pivotal

'The stone the builders rejected has become the capstone' (v. 10).

In Mark 12 Jesus gives the religious leaders a complete answer to their question about his authority, but not in the direct way they expect. He tells a poignant parable with obvious implications. The parable uses a setting familiar to people of Jesus' day. It had been used in Old Testament times as well (Psalm 80; Isaiah 5).

It wasn't unusual for cultivated land to have an absentee landlord. Besides the trained vines, the vineyard Jesus describes has everything requisite for success. Its boundaries are marked. It has a vat for collection of the juice pressed from grapes. The tower is for wine storage, quarters for workers and as a look-out against robbers at harvest time.

Jesus' hearers don't need an explanation of the characters. The vineyard represents Israel; it belongs to God. The tenant cultivators are the rulers of Israel throughout history. The owner's servants whom he sends to check on the vineyard and receive his share of its profits represent prophets. The owner's son is Jesus.

The drama illustrates several things about God. He is generous and wise in his provision, he is trusting in his delegation, he is patient in his dealings with those to whom he's entrusted his work but in the end his justice prevails.

Through the story Jesus reveals several things about himself. First, he is not one of the prophets, but the Son, the Messiah. Next, he says he knows he will be killed, but he knows he will finally triumph. The tragic tale also says that although people don't think God cares what they do, he does and he will call us to account for what we do with our privileges and our knowledge. The story is too much for the religious leaders. Jesus must be stopped.

The psalm (118) Jesus quotes to close his parable may have originally applied to Israel – the nation rejected by world powers but which held a key role in history. But Jesus applied it to himself and the Church continued to see the stone rejected by the builders which became the living keystone, the essential finishing piece of the structure – as the resurrected Christ (1 Peter 2:4–8). So may we.

Psalm 119 – a Primer

'God's Word is better than a diamond, better than a diamond set between emeralds. You'll like it better than strawberries in spring, better than red, ripe strawberries' (Psalm 19:10, MSG).

At a used-book sale I found a set of early American readers. The first was a primer designed to help children learn basic letters and words. It gave practical advice and reflected Christian doctrine. Beside the letter B and a sketch of a Bible it read: 'Thy life to mend this book attend.' The maxims and illustrations went from A to Z.

Many editions of the *New England Primer* contained a poem attributed to the English Protestant clergyman and commentator, John Rogers, who was martyred for his faith in the mid-sixteenth century. Part of the first verse of the parting poem he wrote for his children says:

> Lay up his laws within your heart,
> And print them in your thought.

Some forms of poetry challenge the brightest poets. A particular structure, prescribed number of lines or rhymes dictates form. Psalm 119 uses the alphabetical form. Could Psalm 119 be seen as a primer of sorts? There are twenty-two sections which follow the twenty-two letters of the Hebrew alphabet. Each section has eight verses. Some call it an octuple acrostic.

To get a sense of what writing this 176-verse psalm must have entailed, we might take the letters of our alphabet and try writing eight lines that begin with each letter, all the while basing the poem on a single unifying subject.

The overarching theme of Psalm 119 is esteem for the Word of God, which reveals God's will for us. Since we love him, we love his Word. As such it is a particularly good psalm to consider on Sundays, as we will throughout this edition.

Synonyms for God's revealed will used throughout Psalm 119 seem to spring from verses 7–9 of David's Psalm 19, today's passage.

Final Answer

'And they were utterly amazed at him' (v. 17, NRSV).

Through his parable of the vineyard Jesus warned those who questioned his credentials, yet the Sanhedrin again sends representatives to try to bait and entrap him by his words. The Sanhedrin, on balance more Pharisees than Sadducees, comprised acting and former high priests, members of priestly families, tribal heads and legalists.

In their campaign against Jesus, the Sanhedrin mix Herodians in with their own delegation of Pharisees – liberals with conservatives. The Herodian Jews support Herod the Great and favour Roman rule, whereas the Pharisees are Jewish purists who resist Roman intervention. Normally the two groups do not agree. But in the common cause of getting rid of Jesus, they work together. Their question about paying taxes is well devised.

They begin with well-chosen flattery to hide their motives. They address Jesus as Teacher and claim to know that he is a man of integrity, impartiality and a teacher of God's truth. In the literal translation of verse 14, the phrase 'because you pay no attention to who they are' carries the idea of not sizing up people by their faces or appearance.

Their real question is should Jews pay tax to Rome. They mean the one-denarius poll tax Rome levied on men and women up to age sixty-five. No one liked taxes; some Jewish revolutionaries violently opposed the domination such taxes represented. If Jesus says paying taxes is lawful, he'll look cowardly and lose popular support. If he says it isn't lawful, the religious leaders will report him to the Roman authorities and he'll be arrested.

Jesus asks for the very coin the poll tax requires and then asks whose name and picture are stamped on it. It's the emperor's. Now contrary to what his entrappers said about his not judging by faces, Jesus sizes up a situation by someone's face – the one on the coin. Jesus doesn't merely advise that tax is a duty but that, more importantly, people made in God's image should give themselves to God. The delegation is dumbfounded at his final answer.

7

The Crux of the Matter

'He is the God of the living' (v. 27, NLT).

Next it's the Sadducees' turn to try to discredit Jesus. Although not as large as the Pharisee bloc, their group holds power, especially relating to the temple. Some of their aristocratic intellectuals arrogantly approach the prophet from the Galilean back country with a debate question they probably are accustomed to using to disparage the Pharisees' belief in the resurrection.

Jesus doesn't debate about the 'what ifs' of who would be the real afterlife husband of a sevenfold widow, but goes to the centre of their error – ignorance both of Scripture and the power of God. The two go hand-in-hand. Scripture brings us to knowledge of God and the Spirit of God brings the Scripture to life.

Jesus begins with the assumption that the Creator has the power to craft a new order of life. He says that when the dead rise, they enter that new order of resurrected life where there is no more death and marriage is no longer necessary. In that respect, he says, people will share a trait with angels. The Sadducees wouldn't like this answer since they denied the existence of angels as well as the resurrection.

Sadducees held the Torah, the first five books of the Bible, to be the only Scripture. Since that was their complete basis of belief and they didn't see immortality described in it, they didn't believe in it. Sadducees held that death meant extinction. Jesus points to their prized books of Moses to correct them.

For example, at the burning bush when God said, 'I am the God of . . . Abraham, Isaac and Jacob', patriarchs who had died long before, he implied his continued relationship with them (Exodus 3:6). For Jesus, the basis of belief in life after death is God's character.

Besides holding a skewed view of heaven, the Sadducees missed out on the rich progressive revelation of God throughout the Old Testament, not to speak of God's superlative revelation right in front of them, the Christ. No wonder Christ flatly says: 'He is not the God of the dead, but of the living. You are badly mistaken!' (Mark 12:27). Our day's scepticism about life after death isn't new. We still need Jesus' correction and his assurance.

Kingdom Borderland

*'The Lord your God is one; so love the Lord God with all your passion
and prayer and intelligence and energy' (vv. 29, 30, MSG).*

When we are between assignments, our perspective begins to shift as we gradually look less on what is ending and more toward what is coming. In this passage, only Jesus is fully aware that these are his last precious days before his death. The questions keep coming. He continues to pay attention to people and give thoughtful replies.

Matthew's account of the encounter in today's reading adds the detail that the Pharisees sent their legal expert after they heard that Jesus had silenced the Sadducees with his answer about the resurrection. Did they seek to upstage others or trip up Jesus? Mark's account says that the lawyer himself heard the Sadducees' interchange with Jesus. Christ's fitting answer prompted the man's question.

The scribes of Jesus' day considered that there were more than only the Ten Commandments. They could identify more than 600 in the Mosaic law. They sometimes tried to summarise all of them with one overarching statement. We can imagine their protracted discussions.

In this light the questioner asks the obviously wise, well-informed rabbi, Jesus, about the nature of the primary commandment. Jesus gives a twofold reply, a brilliant new combination that distils the essence of human moral obligation: God is unique, so choose to love God with every part of your being and others as yourself.

The lawyer heartily endorses this answer. When he enthusiastically adds: 'Why, that's better than all offerings and sacrifices put together!' (v. 33, *MSG*), Jesus is pleased that the man is beginning to embrace the gospel. 'When Jesus realized how insightful he was, he said, "You're almost there, right on the border of God's Kingdom"' (v. 34, *MSG*). With such encouragement from Christ we can hope that the man became his true follower.

If we rely on God, the Spirit of Christ will prompt us as well with the answer that draws sincere seekers to the kingdom.

9

God Knows

'All the others gave what they'll never miss; she gave extravagantly what she couldn't afford – she gave her all' (v. 44, MSG).

Finally the questions end. Since the religious leaders haven't stumped Jesus and some of their members are actually being won over by him, they stop before they're humiliated further. They'll think of another way to trap him.

Now Jesus turns things around with a question which confounds and dumbfounds them. He quotes Psalm 110 and asks how David can call the Son of David his Lord. He is correcting a prevalent misconception. The Messiah people expected from David's lineage would be a human liberator. Anyone who could free them politically would seem heaven-sent. Jesus teaches that the Christ is more than that, he's actually David's Lord. The Messiah brings people to God.

As Jesus poses such new ideas that no one contradicts, the crowd listens with delight. Jesus finishes his teaching in this part of the temple with a warning to be on guard against religious opportunists among the teachers of sacred law. They like to make an impression by what they wear, by who greets them with respect, and by preferential seating in synagogues and at feasts.

Jesus says they devour widows' houses. It is easy for the unscrupulous to prey on the most vulnerable. Some of those who practise it in the first century use religion to justify inveigling others to support them. Jesus strongly condemns their ostentatious behaviour, their greed and their long showy prayers with which they attempt to cloak it. He leaves no doubt that God will punish them severely.

Jesus moves from teaching in the court of the Gentiles. He sits in the court of the women, where trumpet-shaped offering containers line a wall. He observes the Passover crowd's giving. Among the masses he sees one poor widow, possibly one who has been defrauded, and notes her rich heart. Mark concludes the section of intense question sessions with this simple reminder about the cost of giving: God knows our resources and our hearts.

Short-Term Forecast . . . Difficult

'And be sure of this: I am with you always, even to the end of the age'
(Matthew 28:20, NLT).

The public teaching in the temple is over. Jesus and the disciples leave for the nearby hills. Someone among them calls attention to the temple's impressive architecture and massive building materials. The white marble glistens and the gold glimmers in the Mediterranean sun.

Jesus isn't dazzled. He sees what others miss. He saw one poor woman among the Passover throng, now he sees beyond the glittering temple exterior to what lies ahead for the temple and for Israel. Jesus tells his incredulous disciples that what they're looking at as grand and permanent will be demolished. Of course they want to know when. Four of them wait to ask him until they reach the Mount of Olives.

In this setting from which they can look back over the city, Jesus explains what they can expect in the near and distant future. Time is almost suspended as the chapter mixes the two forecasts. Bible commentator William Barclay reminds us that the Olivet discourse is tricky for us to understand because much of what Jesus says reflects Jewish ideas and teaching well known in that day but unfamiliar to us.

The disciples combine their question about when the temple would be destroyed with what will signal the start of the Messianic age. Jesus starts with the second part by warning against those who would warp the truth to suit themselves as well as against false 'signs' and misinterpretation of events. We continue to need such alerts as well as the principles of facing opposition to our faith.

Christ's short-term forecast of things his followers will face seems disconcerting. Yet while they can anticipate persecution and rejection, Jesus assures them that nevertheless the gospel will spread (v. 10). Further, the Holy Spirit will not desert them, but will aid them (v. 11). His encouragement remains for us in our circumstances too.

Long-Term Forecast . . . Promising

'Sky and earth will wear out; my words won't wear out' (v. 31, MSG).

During the communiqué in Mark 13, when Jesus speaks about what comes in the last days and precedes his second coming, he uses word pictures familiar to the disciples. Apocalyptic literature and prophecy from half a dozen Old Testament books had formed popular Jewish thought about the 'day of the Lord'.

Jesus prophesies about wars, famines and earthquakes. Those things begin to play out a short time later, and still do. He also speaks of unnatural disasters that defy human explanation – things that take place in the heavens. What he says in Mark 13:24–25 is reminiscent of Isaiah 13:10 and 34:4. The sun and moon go dark, stars shower down on the earth. Finally, when Christ returns in the clouds, everyone sees him.

We do not know what all of the imagery means or when Christ will return. Jesus, who limited his own knowledge of many things while on earth, tells his followers that only the Father knows when he'll return. But we do know that the Lord will come again.

Mark finishes the chapter with a story Jesus tells about staying ready. In a modern variation on that theme, I recall a family memory. It happened before the days of mobile phones, much less the Internet or GPS receivers. Our young family took an affordable summer holiday, a camping trip. A co-worker agreed to house-sit while we were away. When our tent collapsed on us after a week in the rain, we packed up our soggy kit and headed home a few days early. The usually unflappable Philip answered the door in shock. He had obviously counted on a few more days to sort out the dishevelled living areas and do a week's worth of washing-up!

The 'Little Apocalypse', as the Olivet Discourse is sometimes called, helps us to deal with the present more than predict the future. Jesus hands out neither maps nor timetables but says: 'What I say to you I say to all, "Be on the alert!"' (v. 37, *NASB*). Staying ready and being faithful is essential now and rewarding in the future. If it is our desire, God will help us. We can count on his word.

A – Aleph

'Happy are those whose way is blameless, who walk in the law of the LORD'
(v. 1, NRSV).

The Psalms comprised the hymnal used in Jewish worship. It was used along with other hymns and songs as the music of first-century Christian worship. Some churches continue to systematically incorporate psalms in their liturgy.

As we examine Psalm 119 we will notice several words used for aspects of God's revealed will:

- God's law (Torah) – his direction or instruction;
- God's testimonies – principles for living;
- God's precepts – rules of conduct;
- God's statutes – social regulations;
- God's commandments – religious principles;
- God's ordinances – right judgements that function in relationships;
- God's Word – his declared will by promises and decrees;
- God's righteousness – his standard for what is right;
- God's truth or faithfulness – which lasts forever;
- Variations of other synonyms for God's way, path or pattern.

We see these terms spread throughout the psalm.

Matthew Henry says Psalm 119 could be considered to be the believer's testimony. The source of our happiness is that through God's mercy in Christ we are forgiven of sin. We are gladdest as we live in accord with what the Holy Spirit says to our hearts, kept blameless through believing God's Word and daily depending on his promises.

Which verse of the opening section of eight verses sets the tone for the psalm for you? For me it's verse 2: 'Happy are they who follow his injunctions, giving him undivided hearts' (*JMT*) or 'who seek, inquire for and of him and crave him with the whole heart' (*AB*). It reminds me of what Jesus quotes from Deuteronomy when he says the commandment of guiding principle is: 'Love the Lord your God with all your heart and with all your soul and with all your mind' (Matthew 22:37). With that intent we can ask with the psalmist for what we know God will do: always attend us.

13

Let's Be Clear

1 Corinthians 14–16

Introduction

At the close of August, we spent time with the exquisite chapter on love (1 Corinthians 13) which reminded us that the Christian's raison d'être is to be like Christ – Love incarnate. While we're still humming that hymn of love, Paul returns to further instruction raised in part by some of the Corinthians' questions. Among other things he challenges their thinking about spiritual gifts, inclusive worship, the resurrection of believers and the grace of giving.

Although not disparaging the gift of tongues, Paul draws attention to the Corinthians' abuse of it and their larger-than-life fascination with this gift. Since spiritual gifts are meant to benefit the whole Church, he points out that a gift such as proclamation of the Word is preferable.

Basically, worship should not be selfish and should be intelligible. Perhaps today Paul might address diverse worship styles or effectively including immigrant believers in orderly worship when their first language differs from that of the host church.

'To sum this up: When you speak forth God's truth, speak your heart out. Don't tell people how they should or shouldn't pray when they're praying in tongues that you don't understand. Be courteous and considerate in everything' (1 Corinthians 14:39–40, *MSG*).

Corinthians saw themselves as cutting-edge believers. Paul addresses their elitism with some specific advice about Christian living in the context of their time and location. As we ask the Holy Spirit's guidance, the Word's timeless principles will help us to think more clearly too.

Words Fail Me

'The one who prays using a private "prayer language" certainly gets a lot out of it, but proclaiming God's truth to the church in its common language brings the whole church into growth and strength' (v. 4, MSG).

Right from the start of chapter 14 Paul clearly states the primacy of living love, of developing whatever gifts God gives us and of proclaiming the truth. In this context he addresses an issue the fledgling independent-minded Corinthian church faced – a proper perspective on what for them had become a prized spiritual gift, speaking in tongues.

He does not devalue the ecstatic private prayer language that some in today's church still consider helpful. Who hasn't occasionally been at a loss for words in prayer or praise? He doesn't ban it entirely from Corinthian Christian gatherings, but reins in its public practice with the harness of interpretation.

I first heard glossolalia in my student days when a small Christian group met regularly for prayer. As an impressionable adolescent, I assumed that the devoted students who prayed in what to me were unintelligible syllables had found a special in-road to God. When a prominent student leader became gravely ill, the group held all-night prayer vigils for her certain recovery. When Faye died I no longer idealised those who prayed in tongues.

Paul says that although its exercise may enhance the individual's spiritual life, it doesn't do much to build up the body of believers (v. 4). Because of its unusual nature, ecstatic spiritual speech can foster pride in the speaker and envy in those hearing such unique speech. No wonder Paul advises people with the gift to reserve it for private devotion.

Paul calls for order and procedure in worship. Ecstatic speech isn't the only issue that can cause dissension and confusion among believers or can put off those looking in from outside the Christian faith. We might think of current concerns that face our churches.

———

To pray:

Lord, help us to discern any hindrances to your gospel.

Five Intelligible Words

'If I don't address you plainly with some insight or truth or proclamation or teaching, what help am I to you?' (v. 6, MSG).

Although speaking in unknown tongues (glossolalia) is not a learned language such as French or Chinese, thinking about situations in which we're exposed to other languages could help. When someone is speaking a language we don't understand, we may not recognise the words, but we often can discern the attitude and spirit of the speaker by the tone, volume or intensity of what they say as well as by non-verbal clues such as body language and cultural context. We don't grasp the particulars, but we know if they're distressed or delighted. We might deduce a need, but we probably won't know how to meet it.

Paul uses a musical illustration. If the notes played or scales used sound strange or dissonant to our ears, we aren't going to be able to hum the tune later. Save that music for targeted special occasions. New tunes should be capable of being easily learned and sung if we intend people to remember them. 'Since you're so eager to participate in what God is doing, why don't you concentrate on doing what helps everyone in the church?' (v. 12, *MSG*).

In an attempt to provide balance, Paul compares special prayer language with another gift, that of proclaiming the truth. From the start of the chapter Paul urges plain proclamation of the gospel message and says it is more beneficial to everyone than using unknown prayer language, however helpful that might be privately. 'But when I'm in a church assembled for worship, I'd rather say five words that everyone can understand and learn from than say ten thousand that sound to others like gibberish' (v. 19, *MSG*).

Verse 3 gives the aim of proclamation or a teaching, preaching ministry: to build up our knowledge of the truth in Christ and enable us to live it out; to encourage us to keep growing and to comfort us: 'But when you proclaim his truth in everyday speech, you're letting *others* in on the truth so that they can grow and be strong and experience his presence with you' (*MSG*). May the Lord help us each to find ways to do precisely that.

The Service of Order

'For God is not a God of disorder but of peace' (v. 33).

Paul says it's fine to be as inarticulate as infants regarding evil, but regarding spiritual understanding the Corinthians should stop being childish (v. 20). He corrects the Corinthians for overrating what they find fascinating but others find confusing: speaking in tongues.

He emphasises the primacy of the message of the gospel which benefits both believers and unbelievers (v. 22). When the truth of the Word is clearly taught, several things are sure to happen. It convicts of sin, discloses judgement, probes a soul's secrets and brings people to bow their hearts before God (vv. 24, 25).

The type of first-century church service Paul describes seems more spontaneous and egalitarian than those in later centuries after a professional clergy developed. The Bible commentator William Barclay reminds us: 'It is a mistake to think that only the professional ministry can ever bring God's truth to men.'[1]

Possibly due to where the gatherings were held or the number who attended, the first-century order of service also seems flexible. I have attended a couple of Friends (Quaker) services in which even the seating was arranged to accommodate everyone's orderly participation. Those may have been rather like what Paul supports for the fledgling house churches. People gather to contribute, not simply to receive. It has its dangers – especially when someone talks too much. Paul addresses that as well when he advises them to thoughtfully take turns (vv. 30–33).

Considering differences in cultural and music preferences, ages in the congregation, the placement of furnishings and a multitude of other factors, it could be helpful to consider how the worship we regularly participate in elevates the proclamation of the Word and provides opportunity for everyone's participation.

'When we worship the right way, God doesn't stir us up into confusion; he brings us into harmony. This goes for all the churches – no exceptions' (v. 33, *MSG*).

What's the Point?

'Don't, by the way, read too much into the differences here between men and women' (11:10, MSG).

Paul is not prohibiting women from praying or speaking in worship. In chapter 11 he gave guidelines for their respectful participation. Scripture clearly supports female proclamation, inspiration, administration, teaching, sacrificial living, discernment, evangelism, courageous spiritual obedience, leadership, hospitality – in a word, ministry.

Some commentators hold that what Paul says in this section addresses an issue with certain Corinthian women who tended to throw off propriety and needed Paul's advice more than once. Although most think these were married women, we don't know for certain, since the word used for women can mean single, married or widowed women.

Paul advises female believers in Corinth not to publicly evaluate the proclamations of others while at worship, but reserve judgement for later private discussion. This instruction ties with his counsel in preceding verses for participants to exercise self-control so that peace and order is maintained in the worshipping assembly and the church is edified.

Although Paul sees all believers as one in Christ, in first-century society women were second-class citizens. Since the fledgling Corinthian church was surrounded by a society with lax morals, he wants to ensure that nothing believers do brings any suspicion of dishonourable living to the way of Christ.

He ends with the rule of not quenching but enabling spiritual gifts, all the while keeping worship orderly and building up the church. If we apply the principle to our own place of worship, perhaps we can identify ways of increasing the effective witness of the church today. Inclusive, harmonious, edifying worship is the point.

———

To pray:

Lord, help us to please you with our worship.

He Lives!

'Christ died for our sins . . . He was buried, and he was raised from the dead on the third day, just as the Scriptures said' (vv. 3, 4, NLT).

Paul must have heard through a third party that some of the Corinthian believers didn't embrace the idea of their own resurrection. So he begins by reminding them that the essential gospel message they had embraced and taken their stand for had not changed. Continuing to hold onto it was crucial to their continued salvation (v. 2). Paul had reminded the Corinthians of the centrality of Christ crucified; he now adds that Christ resurrected is basic to Christian belief. By extension, all believers' resurrection hinges on it.

That Christ was resurrected was attested to by hundreds of eye-witnesses, many of whom were still living as Paul wrote and could verify that after his crucifixion they had seen the living Christ. Three of those mentioned were Early Church leaders. William Barclay finds Paul's mention of Peter and James poignant. Both had disappointed Jesus, yet he appeared to them after his resurrection.

Peter denied Christ, then wept aloud and lamented with remorse. The angel told the women at the empty tomb at Easter to let the disciples and Peter know they would see Jesus (Mark 16:7). Luke says that the disciples told the men who returned from their Easter encounter with Jesus on the road to Emmaus that Jesus had appeared to Simon (24:34). Jesus brought the one who caused him pain, comfort. 'Love can go no further than to think more of the heartbreak of the man who wronged it than of the hurt it itself has received.'[2]

James, brother of Jesus, did not believe in him during his ministry. Jesus' brothers were hostile towards him and thought he was insane. But Jesus met James more than halfway and he became Christ's loyal follower, even being martyred for his faith. Paul includes himself as one of those who had disappointed Christ, but to whom he appeared after his resurrection (1 Corinthians 15:8, 9). The encounter was Paul's conversion and beginning of an incredibly arduous and rewarding apostleship journey.

To ponder:

What is the significance of our resurrected Lord to our own faith?

He Is or We Aren't

'If you became believers because you trusted the proclamation that Christ is alive, risen from the dead, how can you let people say that there is no such thing as a resurrection?' (v. 12, MSG).

The Corinthians' disbelief in a personal resurrection reflected a philosophy prevalent in Greek society. It allowed for the immortality of the disembodied soul. Since matter was scorned and the body discounted, immortality involved escape from the source of all weakness – the body. Even the Jewish concept of life after death had only progressed from despair to glimmers of hope.

Paul's view is different from either. The human body is not evil or Jesus wouldn't have inhabited one. In his resurrected state, Jesus was recognisable. Christian belief holds that the life to come is designed for the total person. In the life to come, individuals retain their personalities. Everything of the body and soul needed for that survives, albeit in a very different state from on earth.

Because Christ was raised from the dead and promised that believers would be too, as Christians we either accept the possibility of our resurrection or reject his. Ours relies on his and his anticipates ours (v. 13). Without Christ's resurrection, the good news isn't so good – the message is empty because there's no living Christ. Without Christ's resurrection, our faith is 'smoke and mirrors' (v. 14, *MSG*).

The first believers' choice to worship on the first day of the week celebrated Christ's resurrection. Paul reminds us that all the apostles said Christ had risen. Their message revolved around Christ's death and resurrection. The message of salvation the Corinthians believed depended on the fact of the resurrection.

Without it, their faith was futile and they remained unregenerate sinners. Without it, believers who died had perished and those martyred for their faith had died tragic, hollow deaths. Without the resurrection, Christianity was literally hopeless. 'Truly, if our hope in Christ were limited to this life only we should, of all mankind, be the most to be pitied!' (v. 19, *JBP*). But Christ did rise; we have a great living hope and a gospel full of life-changing power.

B – *Beth*

'I treasure your word in my heart, so that I may not sin against you'
(v. 11, NRSV).

In the second set of eight verses we find many verbs describing the way to live a Word-focused life. The words may vary according to the version we use, but the concepts are the same. If we treasure the Word in our hearts, are eager to learn from it, declare it to others, rejoice in it, reflect on it, take delight in it, we will live by it.

How do we actually do this? It takes time and intention. It's the things we choose to think about more than the motivational posters on our walls that affect our behaviour. It's the Christian, Word-based perspective we bring to what we read and view that helps us sift things out.

It's the time we take with the Word in one way or another, the songs we listen to and replay in our minds, the way we participate in times of public worship and private meditation that set the tone for our attitude towards the Word. These and more contribute to whether we thrive in living by the Word.

When we remember that Jesus is the Word Made Flesh, we could be enriched by substituting his name for references to God's Word. Live according to Jesus (v. 9); hide Jesus in our heart (v. 11); talk about Jesus (v. 13); follow Jesus (v. 14); consider Jesus (v. 15); delight in Jesus and care for the things of Jesus (v. 16).

It could also be a singular blessing to choose a recurring word or phrase and see it used throughout the psalm – for example, 'whole heart'; or as Moffatt's translation puts it, 'undivided heart': 'I give thee an undivided heart; oh never may I stray from thy control!' (v. 10). Amen!

———

To pray:

The General of The Salvation Army calls us to prayer for peace from this Sunday. It is the week in which the United Nations International Day for Peace falls. For the sake of the millions daily affected by conflict in myriad ways, we pray for peace.

First-Fruits

'He won't let up until the last enemy is down – and the very
last enemy is death!' (vv. 25, 26, MSG).

Paul finishes the hypothetical negative suppositions which followed for
those who deny Christ's resurrection. Paul switches to the fact of the
risen Christ from which stem positive consequences for the believer since
the Christian's life and lot are bound up with Christ's.

Paul says our risen Christ has become the 'first-fruits' of those who have
died. The concept of first-fruits was well known. The Old Testament taught
that first-fruits of the harvest belonged to the Lord and should be
presented to him as an offering of gratitude for them and all who would
follow.

The first sheaf of the new crop of barley was presented the day after
Passover Sabbath (see Leviticus 23:11). Isn't it amazing that the first
Easter coincided with that very day? No wonder Paul uses the term 'first-
fruits' to illustrate the risen Lord's position as example, first instalment and
promise of more to come for believers.

Scripture uses the term 'first-fruits' figuratively. In the Old Testament
it represents Israel. In addition to Paul's reference to Christ, in New
Testament Epistles it has been used for initial believers of a certain location
or of all Christians of that original period of the Church. It sometimes
refers to the present blessings of the Holy Spirit which assure greater
blessings yet to come.

Paul shifts to a couple of similes which *The Message* says have 'a nice
symmetry' (v. 21). Death came via a disobedient human being and the
resurrection comes via the obedient God-human, Christ. In Adam all die.
In Christ all can live. Paul details what he means by this in Romans
5:12–19. Human bodies won't be destroyed as some in Corinth claimed.
Rather, Christ will nullify his opponent, the very destroyer of humankind,
death.

In verse 27 of today's reading, Paul refers to Psalm 8:6 and reads it like
the writer does in Hebrews 2:8, 9 – as Messianic and pointing to end times
when everything will be subject to Christ. Come, Lord Jesus!

Future Outlook Shapes Present Life

'Think straight. Awaken to the holiness of life. No more playing fast and loose with resurrection facts' (v. 34, MSG).

After Paul gives the basic order of resurrection – Christ first as example and guarantee, then the dead in Christ at his return for the Church and eventually the final resurrection and judgement – he uses some practical references and warnings that the Corinthians would particularly understand.

There are numerous explanations for Paul's mention of baptism for the dead. Some propose that if it is a local vicarious ritual practised in Corinth, Paul is not endorsing it but using it to point out their flaw in logic if at the same time they denied the resurrection. Even if their custom was mistaken, it assumed belief in immortality.

Some find the reference to baptism a general symbol which connects believers with death and resurrection. Other commentators suggest that what Paul means isn't a baptism of water but of blood. The public symbol of conversion may have been viewed as a risky act, putting a person in danger of martyrdom, which was prevalent in the first century.

Paul points out that, whether threatened by death or not, Christians were always in jeopardy. Risking one's life in any way for personal earthly motives would have minimal reward. Without hope of resurrection, suffering or dying for one's faith would be unreasonable. We may as well 'eat, drink and be merry'. Without the resurrection, sensual excess, well known in the city of Corinth, could seem justifiable. But the doctrine of the resurrection brings balance and focus.

Paul also warns against the subtle influence of non-believers on Christian doctrine. The reminder holds in our technological age as well. Some Corinthian believers unwittingly bought into arguments denying some tenets of their faith. Wake up! Paul counsels, 'Don't fool yourselves. Don't let yourselves be poisoned by this anti-resurrection loose talk' (v. 33, *MSG*). Don't take anyone's advice which is contrary to the Holy Spirit's. One practical antidote is taking care of the company we keep – even electronically.

Not Renovation, Resurrection

'And we're only looking at pre-resurrection "seeds" – who can imagine what the resurrection "plants" will be like!' (v. 41, MSG).

In C. S. Lewis's fable *The Great Divorce*, things are inexplicable in the life to come. Grass as tough as diamonds doesn't bend underfoot, yet easily bends as a small bird hops on it. Things are quite unexpected for Lewis's characters who leave earth for the afterlife.

After Paul establishes how important the reality of resurrection is to the overall plan of redemption, he addresses some questions that remain for the Corinthians. Their questions could be ours: how are the dead raised and what is the nature of the resurrected body?

Paul tries to express the indescribable by using ordinary illustrations to express the principles of extraordinary resurrected life. Although it is unusual for Paul to use metaphors from nature in his Epistles, he does so here to illustrate the resurrection. We may not understand the process completely, but everyone who plants small dry seeds and watches new green plants sprout from the soil knows that the new plant emerges on condition that the seed dies.

Says William Barclay: 'At one and the same time, there can be dissolution, difference and continuity. Our earthly bodies will dissolve; they will rise again in very different form; but it is the same person who rises. It is still we who exist.'[3]

Paul turns to animal life. We're acquainted with the wide variety of living organisms – human, animal, bird, fish – which God created. Can't we infer that he is unrestricted in creating another aspect of life – resurrection life? God who created and governs the process of new life in plants and animals surely exercises power over people's heaven-suited bodies as well.

For one more illustration Paul points to the sky. The celestial bodies God created are particularly splendid and very different from what he created on earth. God's power is limitless and can't be measured by our comprehension. Jesus reminds us that what is impossible with humans is possible with God (Mark 10:27).

Transformed

'But there's far more to life for us. We're citizens of high heaven! We're
waiting the arrival of the Saviour, the Master, Jesus Christ, who will
transform our earthy bodies into glorious bodies like his own'
(Philippians 3:20, MSG).

After stating differences between creation's earthly and celestial bodies
and suggesting that our mortal bodies are different from our future
resurrection bodies, Paul offers more contrasts.

What we have now in this fallen world is perishable; what we will have
is permanent. What we have now is affected in various ways by the miseries
sin brought to our world and the human condition; what we will have is no
longer subject to those threatening downward pulls. What we have now
declines with age and is feeble, even in the most fit; what we will have
knows no such limitations. What we have now is well-designed for life on
planet earth – a body animated by a soul; what we will have is a body
appropriate for the new dimension of life in heaven – a body suited to the
spirit's activity.

According to Paul, it follows that if there is a natural body, there is a
spiritual one as well. He traces their origins – Adam and Christ. God made
Adam and all his descendants with a body and soul. Christ is the founder
of a new order – spiritual people whose ultimate nature is the resurrected
life. Natural, earthy life comes to all, but spiritual, heavenly life comes only
by choice through Christ.

Such spiritual life is not only for the future; it impacts and marks our
earthly lives now. As 'we've worked from our earthy origins, let's embrace
our heavenly ends' (v. 49, *MSG*).

We accept our God-given body with its wonders, distinctiveness, yet
limitations. As believers we also bear the image of Christ and by God's
grace know triumph over sin and death (Romans 5:17). One day he'll
make us beautiful and whole when he puts everything as it should be under
and around him (Philippians 3:21). We, who belong to Christ, will gain a
spiritual body like Christ's.

Paul doesn't go further about the spiritual body. It is enough to say that
God who formed us transforms us with what we need. Hallelujah!

So Then . . .

'But now in a single victorious stroke of Life, all three – sin, guilt, death – are gone, the gift of our Master, Jesus Christ. Thank God!' (v. 57, MSG).

To cap all that the apostle says about resurrection, he ends the section gladly exalting in death's defeat and Christ's victory.

Since he's established that temporary flesh and blood isn't fit for an eternal heavenly existence and that believers who die are transformed, he addresses a question the Corinthians may have had. What happens to those who are living at the time of Christ's return? Those bodies, even if not dissolved by death, would need to be changed too. Precisely!

Paul says something similar to what he'd written in his first letter to the Thessalonians (4:15–17). He introduces a mystery, unknown in Old Testament times but now a divinely disclosed open secret: we will all be instantly changed (1 Corinthians 15:51–53). Our newly organised bodies will be suited to heaven's environment, yet retain recognisable personal identity.

Paul alludes to Old Testament passages in Isaiah and Hosea about God swallowing death and death coming to an end. For all who trust in Christ, when sin and death's hold is completely broken through him, the redemptive work of God finishes in total triumph.

The word 'victory' launches Paul into something of a 'hallelujah wind-up', to use an early-day Salvation Army term. 'To Paul, victory over sin and the reality of the resurrection were the towering peaks of redemption.'[4]

From his stance on those twin peaks and full of the hope they offer, Paul urges us to their practical results: staying faithful – especially during times of opposition or difficulty – and doing more than the minimum requirement, because such a life amounts to something. The goal is worthy of our best efforts.

Or as John Wesley states it: 'Whatever you do for his sake shall have its full reward in that day. Let us also endeavour, by cultivating holiness in all its branches, to maintain this hope in its full energy.'[5] Amen.

Grace-filled Giving

'Keep your eyes open, hold tight to your convictions, give it all you've got, be resolute, and love without stopping' (vv. 13, 14, MSG).

How would we finish a letter of correction and instruction? As well as giving a final blessing Paul ends this letter with practical matters that benefit Christian concord. Although not as breathtaking as thoughts of resurrection, helping other believers in need is essential to Christian fellowship. Paul asks the Corinthians to give for the saints at Jerusalem.

Apparently the concept of holding all things in common, prevalent at first in the Jerusalem church (Acts 2:22), was no longer in vogue. Augustine suggests that some in Jerusalem may have indeed slipped into poverty due to their initial keenness for communal ownership. Adam Clarke posits that persecution by the Jews ruined the Jerusalem believers financially. G. Campbell Morgan sees their poverty-stricken state as coming in part from their failure to evangelise until persecution forced them out of Jerusalem.

Paul doesn't speculate about the cause of their deficiencies, but he knows that all believers are indebted to the Church, which began in Jerusalem. He had instructed the churches in Galatia to take a collection for the saints at Jerusalem. He asks the Corinthians to do the same. This is beyond their local church needs.

Whether for local or distant ministry, Paul emphasises the principle of regular giving. He supports intentional giving of a portion of whatever income we receive. Although he leaves the amount or percentage to the individual, he knows that the principle of regular giving affects the giver.

Even if the sum amounts to the same thing in the end, systematic, consistent, voluntary giving is preferable to occasional grudging pressured giving in reaction to emotional appeals. We're more likely to give exuberantly and sacrificially if our giving is a response to God's grace to us.

At the end of a letter of correction, Paul promises to visit his readers and urges them to be steadfast and loving for the Lord is coming. He invokes the grace of Christ on them and assures them of his love.

G – Gimel

'Happy are they who live uprightly, living by the Eternal's law!' (v. 1, JMT).

In this section the psalmist says that both the aim and vital support of life is knowing and doing God's will. It offers vision, guidance and a goal. It sounds like the testimony of one who, through some type of adversity, has seen the entire cache of usual earthly crutches removed and knows what it is to rely utterly on God and his Word.

Depending on the translation of the Hebrew word *ger* in verse 19, the psalmist refers to himself as a stranger on earth or in these parts, a foreigner in the land, a sojourner on earth, an alien on earth, or a resident alien in the land. Whichever word we use, it seems to mean someone who is from elsewhere and therefore doesn't automatically fit in.

An amazing amount of rudimentary knowledge about how we should correspond to our surroundings is transferred to even the youngest child almost from infancy. Without such knowledge we're apt to say or do something that embarrasses us or others. When we move from our birth culture to a different one, language is one obvious change we consider, but what about customs, courtesies, appropriate behaviour in various settings? It's wonderful to find a guidebook written by someone who has experienced the changes between cultures and can help to steer us.

The psalmist senses that God has the guidebook for people who are citizens of heaven but at present live on earth. That's the idea behind verse 19: 'Hide not thy commands from me, an alien on the earth' (*JMT*). God's Word is the ultimate survival guide.

To pray:

Join the worldwide Salvation Army today in praying on behalf of those who work to combat the evil of sex-trade trafficking. We also pray for the victims and the survivors of the trafficking.

From Slavery to Freedom

A study from Exodus by guest writer
Major Max Sturge

Introduction

The book of Exodus develops the story of God's promise to Abraham: 'I will make you into a great nation . . . and all peoples on earth will be blessed through you' (Genesis 12:2, 3). But Genesis ends with God's people, the Israelites, in Egypt rather than in the Promised Land. Exodus opens with the Pharaoh of Egypt making them slaves. How could a bunch of motley slaves be a blessing to the world?

Through Moses, God (Yahweh) sets his people free. God's redemption of Israel from slavery becomes the Old Testament paradigm for the salvation from sin later procured for us by our Lord and Saviour, Jesus Christ.

In Exodus we encounter the holy, glorious God of the universe who chooses to tabernacle with his often unholy people. As 'a kingdom of priests and a holy [people]' (19:6), their responsibility is to mediate their knowledge of the one true God to the world. The story concludes with the glory of God, a manifestation of his holiness, filling the tabernacle (Exodus 40).

Exodus reminds us that we worship and serve a God whose incomparable holiness should fill us with awe and who deserves our obedient love and utter devotion. In the fuller revelation of the New Testament, this majestic God, by his Spirit, indwells the followers of Jesus, makes them his holy people and empowers them for his mission in the world.

Major Max Sturge is Associate Editor of Salvationist, *a publication of the Canada and Bermuda Territory. Max and his wife, Doreen, served for six years at the college for officer training in St John's, Newfoundland and Labrador, and twenty-seven years in corps ministry. He says his most satisfying responsibility has been preaching and teaching the Word of God.*

Trusting God in the Darkness

'All peoples on earth will be blessed through you' (12:3).

The Bible is a story, the unfolding drama of redemption. Our first parents, Adam and Eve, disobeyed God. The spiritual virus of prideful independence and disobedience infected their offspring. Eventually their descendants became so increasingly disrespectful of God's way for right living that God, wanting to start over with a new humanity, destroyed with a flood all living things on earth – except for Noah and his family.

How would God create a new humanity who would obey his rules? After many centuries of repopulating the earth God covenanted with Abraham: 'I will make you a great nation . . . and all peoples on earth will be blessed through you' (12:2, 3). He later promised Abraham and his descendants land in which to settle. But what is that 'blessing'? How Abraham's descendants become a blessing to the world is the story of the rest of the Bible.

Genesis closes with a famine in the Promised Land forcing Abraham's descendants to migrate to Egypt for survival. 'But, God, you promised us this land. Why are you now forcing us to go to Egypt?' they asked.

When upsetting things happen to us we might likewise question: 'God, this doesn't make sense. What are you up to?' In the present we often don't see God's purposes, but months or even years later we can make sense out of what is happening in our lives. In the darkness we learn to trust the God we walk with in the light.

Is it possible that in the hard times of your life, when you wonder what God is up to, that he is quietly shaping you into the kind of person he wants you to be – like his Son, Jesus Christ, in character – and at the same time preparing you for eternity with him in the new heaven and new earth (2 Corinthians 3:17, 18; Revelation 21:1)? What a grand purpose and destiny!

To pray:

O God, I pray that life's hardships will make me a winner rather than a whiner, better rather than bitter.

God's Undefeatable Promise

'The more they were oppressed, the more they multiplied' (v. 12).

Exodus opens with Abraham's descendants enslaved in Egypt. How can a bunch of slaves ever be a 'blessing' to the world? They have become 'exceedingly numerous'. In the harshest of circumstances God is keeping his promise to Abraham: 'I will make you into a great nation' (Genesis 12:2). Nothing can ultimately defeat God's promises and his plan for his people to be a blessing to the world.

A dangerous threat emerges. Free Hebrew labour is a huge economic benefit to the Pharaoh's building schemes, but he fears that a large population of Hebrews will threaten his rule and therefore orders the slave masters to make life so miserable for them that they will have fewer children. However, 'the more they were oppressed, the more they multiplied and spread' (v. 12). God reminds his people that no human ruler can prevent God from keeping his promise of making his people a blessing to the world.

The Pharaoh's strategy doesn't work. He decrees that the Hebrew midwives kill all newborn baby boys. Not fearing for their own lives, two midwives courageously ignore the king's order. Later, when he accepts their explanation for letting the boys live – 'Hebrew women are not like Egyptian women; they are vigorous and give birth before the midwives arrive' (v. 19) – he comes across as the most gullible Egyptian Pharaoh of all time.

It isn't uncommon for peculiar beliefs regarding different minority groups to be accepted in a larger society. Maybe it feeds our need to not feel threatened by some groups or simply to feel superior to others. The midwives obviously play upon Egyptian prejudices regarding this Hebrew minority group.

———————

To ponder:

Am I fearful of, or feel superior to, certain cultural minorities in my city or country? Do I thus forfeit the opportunity to be a blessing to them?

31

God's Mysterious and Mischievous Ways

'Nurse him for me, and I will pay you' (v. 9).

Directing the Hebrew midwives to kill the Hebrew boys didn't work, so the Pharaoh ordered all his people: 'Every [Hebrew] boy that is born you must throw into the Nile' (1:22). But God quietly goes to work almost mischievously to undermine the Pharaoh's absolute authority. A baby boy is born to what would later become the priestly family of Levi. His mother hides him for three months and then puts him in a papyrus basket in the River Nile, presumably trusting God to protect him there.

The baby's sister stands 'at a distance to see what would happen to him' (v. 4). How does she feel as she looks at that basket in the river? Who rescues this baby? The Pharaoh's daughter! She realises it is one of the Hebrew babies. The baby is crying. Her nurturing instincts kick in. She ignores her father's edict. When the baby's sister, who happens to be there, offers to recruit one of the Hebrew women to nurse the baby for her, the princess happily agrees. Now the Pharaoh's own daughter has defied his decree!

This Hebrew boy, Moses, would be raised in the court of the Egyptian Pharaoh. Who would nurse and raise him in his initial years and get paid for it? His own mother! But how does his mother feel later when she has to take him to the Pharaoh's daughter to be formally adopted as her royal son? Does she cry herself to sleep for many nights? Does she tell him she is his mother? Having undoubtedly bonded with her, how does Moses feel about having to leave her?

The story is replete with irony: God's promise of Abraham's having numerous descendants is initially fulfilled not in the Promised Land but in oppressive Egypt. Moses is rescued by the daughter of the man who is trying to kill him. He is nursed by his own mother. What is God up to in having Moses raised in the Egyptian court? God moves in mysterious ways, his wonders to perform.

God Keeps His Promises

'I will surely bring you back again' (Genesis 46:4).

In spite of harsh oppression and the Egyptian Pharaoh's attempted population control, God's promise to Abraham of many descendants has indeed been fulfilled. But they are slaves in Egypt. Earlier God promised Abraham's descendant, Jacob/Israel: 'Do not be afraid to go down to Egypt, for I will make you a great nation there. I will go down to Egypt with you, and I will surely bring you back again' (Genesis 46:4). How will God keep the second part of that promise so that a motley bunch of slaves can become a 'blessing' to the world? They need to be set free to be a blessing to others.

Now we know what God was up to in having a son of Hebrew slaves, Moses, raised in the Egyptian court. He would learn invaluable leadership skills from the ruling power of the day. Who better to lead a tribe of freed slaves out of the clutches of the mighty Egyptian Pharaoh than one who was raised and trained in the Egyptian court? Moses would become God's man in a turning point in the history of God's people, in God's saving plan for his people and for the world.

God keeps his promises. 'I will make you a great nation . . . and all peoples on earth will be blessed through you' (Genesis 12:2, 3). What an awesome God we serve – a God we can trust to fulfil his promises for us even when we can't make sense out of the obstacles and heartache invading our lives!

Several years ago, when my wife discovered she had breast cancer, Isaiah 43:1, 2, 5 brought comfort and hope: 'Fear not, for I have redeemed you . . . You are mine . . . When you pass through the waters, I will be with you; when you walk through the fire, you will not be burned . . . Because I love you . . . do not be afraid, for I am with you.' We rejoice in her good health today.

To ponder:

For what do I need to trust God?

God's Leadership School

'I have become an alien in a foreign land' (v. 22).

Moses will become God's man in rescuing his people, but do the leadership skills he learned in Egypt qualify him for the daunting challenge of leading his people out of Egypt into the Promised Land? He observed an Egyptian beating one of his fellow Hebrew kinsmen. Moses 'killed him and hid him in the sand'. Is that the type of leader God wants to use to deliver his people from slavery? When shortly afterwards he tries to break up a fight between two of his own people, he is told: 'Who made you ruler and judge over us? Are you thinking of killing me as you killed the Egyptian?' (v. 14).

Selwyn Hughes, a Welsh Christian minister best known for writing the daily devotional notes *Every Day With Jesus*, has commented that it was natural for Moses to want to do something to aid his kinsmen, but it was done in the pride of his own strength. Moses was too strong. 'God can only entrust his power to those who are humbled and emptied and conscious, not of their power but of their helplessness,' wrote Hughes.

Hearing about the incident, the Pharaoh tries to kill Moses and Moses escapes to the wilderness area of Midian (v. 15). There he rescues the seven daughters of the priest of Midian from belligerent shepherds and humbly helps draw water for their flock. He is learning to balance his strong, aggressive personality with a servant heart. The priest rewards Moses with one of his daughters, Zipporah, as his wife. In Midian he has a son, Gershom (v. 22). The price Moses pays for his hot temper that resulted in murder is his many years in Midian away from his people.

Philip Yancey says:

Moses spent half his life learning leadership skills from the ruling empire of the day and half his life learning wilderness survival skills after fleeing a murder rap. Who better to lead a tribe of freed slaves through the wilderness to the Promised Land?[6]

Isn't it amazing how God can use the painful experiences of our lives to shape us for his great purposes today and mould our characters in preparing us for the world to come?

Yahweh – Our All-Sufficient God

'Go. I am sending you to Pharaoh to bring my people the
Israelites out of Egypt' (v. 10).

Leading an undisciplined bunch of slaves out of Egypt and through an inhospitable wilderness would be a formidable challenge. Who in his right mind would even consider it? Moses knew only too well the mighty power of an autocratic Egyptian Pharaoh and how determined he would be to preserve the considerable economic benefit of free Hebrew labour.

But then God steps in, appearing to Moses through a burning bush that is not consumed by its flames. Moses recognises this God as the God of his forefathers and is terrified to 'look at God' (v. 6). Will God's burning holiness consume Moses if he looks upon God? God tells him the time has come for God to rescue his people from their oppression in Egypt. Moses is shocked out of his sandals!

This intimidating assignment makes Moses feel very inadequate. His response reminds me of that scary sense of inadequacy I felt when God called me to be a Salvation Army officer. How does God address Moses' fears and deficits? By revealing himself to Moses in the form of a new name, Yahweh, meaning 'I am who I am' or 'I will be what I will be', God reveals himself to Moses as the self-existent, all-powerful God, the One who will be what he and his people will need. He will guide them and meet all their needs, including in the wilderness. Have you discovered this awesome God yet, the One who is able to meet all your needs, including in your 'wilderness' times?

Ultimately God will compel the Pharaoh to let his people go; however, he will use Moses as his mouthpiece. God will cause the Egyptians to be generous to the Israelites in giving them jewellery and clothing as they prepare to leave Egypt. The silver and gold will later be used in building the tabernacle in the wilderness. What an honour to partner with God to further his redemptive purposes!

D – *Daleth*

'I run in the path of your commands, for you have set my heart free' (v. 32).

Some Bible statisticians find more multiples of eight beyond the number of verses in each section of the psalm. Some suggest eighty prayers, sixty-four declarations, forty-eight appreciations, eight aspirations and recurring expressions such as 'teach me'. Hebrew language analysts even note multiples of eight in the number of words and letters in the psalm. Although interesting sidelights, they're simply tabulations.

The thoughts the verses convey are more helpful to us. Reading them in different versions is instructive. In today's segment there's a clear progression from discouragement to assurance. First the psalmist gives an honest account of the way he sees his life when depressing days come. Yet when he's low he knows that the only dependable lift for his spirit is God's Word and its sure promises.

He says he's recounted his ways. Literally, he's numbered them. If there were things he'd done wrong or left undone, he's no doubt prayed for forgiveness because he can say that he is confident and grateful that God has heard him (v. 26).

He builds his renewal on this certainty. The psalmist's prayer could be ours: preserve me, teach me, let me thoroughly understand what you say, be gracious to me through clear disclosure of your word, build me up by your word, keep me from deceiving myself.

After focusing on what God can do, he confidently concludes: I choose your truth and remind myself of it at every turn. I am glued to what you say, so don't let me be down. Because you will continue to enlarge my heart's capacity, I will go forward, running on without fear of tripping over things you have removed.

We know times of feeling down, whether because of our choices or our circumstances. Some of us are even affected physically or psychologically by weather patterns. Thinking through the verses of this segment of Psalm 119 can help us to know we will move on, not in our own strength or self-confidence, but in what ultimately counts most – the Lord's assurances.

Closing the Credibility Gap

'I will . . . teach you what to say' (v. 12).

Moses is concerned that his people will not have confidence in him as God's leader and thus will not follow him. God has a unique way of equipping Moses in his leadership school. God promises miraculous 'signs' through him. Consequently the people will believe in him as their leader and in God's message of deliverance through him.

The first sign would be Moses' staff becoming a snake and then turning back into a staff. Staffs and snakes were often seen as Egyptian symbols of power and life. This sign will therefore show Yahweh's power over Egyptian dominance. Next, God will make Moses' hand leprous, then return it to normal. This will highlight Yahweh's power over disease and warn the Pharaoh that his ambassador, Moses, can inflict diseases upon his people.

God tells Moses that if his people will not trust him after these two signs, he is to take some water from the River Nile and throw it on the ground. The water will become blood. This sign will demonstrate Yahweh's power over the Egyptian gods.

With his deep-seated insecurities and awareness of Egypt's military capability, Moses still isn't convinced that he's the man for this daunting task, especially since he's a poor speaker. Even though God gave him his mouth, Moses doesn't feel he can communicate persuasively with his people and with the Pharaoh. 'Case closed! Get off my back, God!' As a last resort God recruits Moses' brother, Aaron, to be the spokesperson. God will speak to Moses, then Moses will convey God's word to Aaron, then Aaron to the people.

Moses finally accepts this formidable commission. After receiving his father-in-law's blessing to leave Midian, Moses goes back with his wife and children to his people in Egypt with the staff of God, the symbol of God's presence and power, in his hand.

To ponder:

What gives a leader credibility with people?

How Do We Measure Success?

*'I will boast all the more gladly about my weaknesses, so that
Christ's power may rest on me' (v. 9).*

Moses' excuses reflected genuine personal inadequacy for the
responsibility to which God called him. When God asks us to do
something he trusts us to get the job done – with his resources and power.
His people need to be set free from slavery to be a blessing to the world;
however, Moses first needs to be set free himself. Set free from being
overwhelmed by his insecurities and weaknesses and ready to trust God to
resource him for this very challenging responsibility.

Do you need to be equipped or re-equipped for the ministry to which
God has called you – whether it's leadership in the home, in the Church,
at work or in the larger world? The one who calls you believes in you. God
believes that, with him as your partner, you can handle it!

As the young scholar-prince, raised and trained in the palace of the
Egyptian Pharaoh, Moses was:

> supremely self-sufficient and attempted single-handedly the deliverance
> of his oppressed fellows. But he was not equipped for God's purpose.
> He was banished from Egypt to undertake a forty-year course in the
> university of the desert. The very excuses he gave to prove his incapacity
> to lead his people were the very resources for God's selection of him for
> the task.
>
> Now, emptied of self-confidence and self-dependence he would lean
> on his God. All through history God has used non-entities because their
> unusual dependence on him left room for the unique display of his
> power. When they are content to be nothing, he can be everything. God
> will not use us in spite of our weakness and inadequacy but because of
> them. He refuses to use our most spectacular gifts and unique
> qualifications until we are ~~weaned from~~ reliance on them. Human
> weakness provides the best backdrop for the display of God's power.[7]

To ponder:

Success is weakness surrendered to God.

Let Freedom Ring!

'Let my people go' (5:1).

The Revd Martin Luther King moved many with his powerful speech to his fellow Americans in 1963:

I have a dream that one day on the red hills of Georgia the sons of former slaves and the sons of former slave owners will be able to sit down together at a table of brotherhood. I have a dream that my four little children will one day live in a nation where they will not be judged by the colour of their skin but by the content of their character . . . Let freedom ring from the snowcapped Rockies of Colorado! . . . Let freedom ring from every hill and every molehill of Mississippi. And . . . when we let freedom ring . . . we will be able to speed up that day when all of God's children, black and white, Jews and Gentiles, Protestants and Catholics, will be able to join hands and sing . . . the old negro spiritual, 'Free at last! Free at last! Thank God Almighty, we are free at last!'

God's call to freedom has echoed through the centuries. It's the message he tells Moses to declare to the mighty Pharaoh of ancient Egypt: 'Let my people go!' The Pharaoh says he does not know the God of Israel, Yahweh, and has no desire to obey this command. A man with many gods, he obviously doesn't have any confidence in a lower-class god of slaves.

He accuses Moses and Aaron of taking the people away from their labour. He increases the people's oppression and requires them to produce just as many bricks as before, but without straw! Why don't Moses and Aaron demonstrate the 'signs' to the Pharaoh in this first visit? They probably want to give him the opportunity to respond voluntarily to their request.

God first lets the Pharaoh choose his own course of action. The Pharaoh will not be able to accuse Israel's God of depriving him of freedom of choice. Similarly, as much as we pray and long for people to repent and turn to Jesus Christ for salvation, we can't force them. And neither does God. He respects human freedom and wants a free and loving response to his Lordship.

The Cost of Leadership

'Why have you brought trouble upon this people?' (5:22).

The Egyptian slave drivers pressure the workers to produce more bricks with less straw. Frustrated and angry, the Israelite foremen appeal to the Pharaoh to reconsider. The Pharaoh accuses them of being lazy. Totally exasperated, they vent their anger on Moses and Aaron: 'May the Lord look upon you and judge you!' Running out of options, Moses complains to God, saying in effect, 'Why have you brought all this trouble upon your people? Why did you recruit me for this impossible task? How are you going to get us out of this mess?'

Leadership can sometimes be frustrating and painful. Have you ever complained to God, 'When are you going to get me out of this mess?' When you run out of options it's never a wrong move to turn to God – though it's usually smarter to turn to him before panic sets in.

Though the Pharaoh rejects the Israelites' request, Yahweh reassures Moses that he will use his mighty power to change the Pharaoh's mind. Moses is probably wondering, 'You think you are going to get this Pharaoh to change his mind? Are we talking about the same Pharaoh?' Perhaps implying that Moses still does not fully grasp the kind of God he is, Yahweh reassures Moses that he is the God of his forefathers, Yahweh, God Almighty, and will keep his covenant promises. By his mighty power he will free them from Egyptian slavery and bring them to the land he promised their forefathers. He will claim them as his special people and be their God. He will be close and available to them.

Do you feel special to God? Do you feel he is close and always available? In the storms of life, do you recall and claim some of his many wonderful promises to boost your spirits and faith?

———————

To ponder:

Why do we grow more, spiritually, in frustrating and painful times than in times of smooth sailing?

God's Evangelistic Method – Mighty Acts of Judgement

'The Egyptians will know that I am the LORD' (7:5).

The brutality of slavery discourages the Israelites so much that they won't listen to Moses any more. Leadership can sometimes severely try our patience with people and with God. God's response to Moses is to repeat his earlier command: 'Go, tell Pharaoh king of Egypt to let the Israelites go out of his country' (6:11). ' "But Lord!" Moses objected, "My own people won't listen to me anymore. How can I expect Pharaoh to listen? I'm such a clumsy speaker!" ' (6:12, *NLT*). God then tells him, in essence, to get on with the job. 'The Lord commanded Moses and Aaron to bring the Israelites out of Egypt' (6:13). Have you been making excuses for not doing what God wants you to do?

How does God compensate for Moses' speaking weakness? Firstly, God tells him that his brother Aaron will do the speaking for him. That problem is fixed. Aaron will relate God's word to Pharaoh. Secondly, God warns him that the Pharaoh will not listen to him, but by mighty acts of judgement God will bring his people out of Egypt. God's miraculous deliverance will cause many Egyptians 'to know that I am the LORD' (7:5).

In short, the miraculous rescue will be evangelistically effective. Some Egyptians will recognise Israel's God, Yahweh, as the incomparable God. This overarching theme is repeated throughout the plagues. These mighty acts of judgement are called 'signs'. They are Yahweh's signs of his superior power over Egypt's gods with the purpose of the people rejecting their inferior gods and embracing Israel's God, Yahweh.

Centuries later, in coming to earth in his Son, Jesus Christ, God's miracles would have a similar evangelistic purpose – to convince people that Jesus is God's Son who can rescue us from the slavery of sin.

Who Hardened Pharaoh's Heart?

'"I will harden Pharaoh's heart" . . . So Pharaoh's heart was hard'
(7:3, 9:35).

The hardening of the Pharaoh's heart is a fascinating theological issue. Initially it appears that he is simply stubborn and will not release the Israelites. Yahweh will therefore have to 'compel' him to do so; however, 7:3, 4 states that Yahweh 'will harden Pharaoh's heart'. God is going to harden Pharaoh's heart, yet compel him to let Israel go? After the first sign, 'Pharaoh's heart became hard and he would not listen' (7:13); similarly after the second, third and fourth signs.

At several points Pharaoh seems to mellow, asks for prayer and acknowledges he has sinned. Yet, when the plagues cease, he changes his mind. In 10:1, 2 the Lord summarises the confrontation for Moses. Yahweh has made the Pharaoh and his officials stubborn; however, this will provide an opportunity for the Lord to demonstrate his superior power to the Egyptians and confirm to the Israelites and their descendants that Yahweh is the one and only Lord.

Was the Pharaoh a mere pawn in God's hands? How do we reconcile the sovereignty of God with human free will?

We find this theological issue later in the New Testament as well. At the Last Supper Jesus refers to Judas: 'The hand of him who is going to betray me is with mine on the table. The Son of Man will go as it has been decreed, but woe to that man who betrays him' (Luke 22:21, 22).

If Judas' betrayal has been decreed by the Father, why is Judas still held accountable for his dastardly action? Peter declares a similar truth on the Day of Pentecost: 'This man [Jesus] was handed over to you by God's set purpose and foreknowledge; and you, with the help of wicked men, put him to death' (Acts 2:23). If Jesus' death was 'by God's set purpose', how could his killers be held responsible for his death? The Bible does not resolve the tension between God's sovereignty and human free will. Instead, it holds them in tension, thus inviting us to acknowledge the mystery.

H – *He*

'GOD, teach me lessons for living so I can stay the course'
(v. 33, MSG). 'I long to obey your commandments! Renew my life
with your goodness' (v. 40, NLT).

The psalmist wants to know and fulfil God's will and way more completely. To that end, in this stanza he asks God to teach him, give him understanding, direct his way, turn his eyes away from the transient and selfish and his heart towards the lasting and selfless, preserve his life, fulfil divine promises and keep him from disgrace, even deserved. We pray that prayer as well.

The poet reveals other reasons connected with staying on track spiritually and then asks for help for these too. He intends to remain faithful, to obey God wholeheartedly, to delight in the things of God, to advance the faith and live a renewed life.

The verb used for 'teach' in verse 33 has the same root as 'torah'. The word essentially means 'direction'. It can be a parent's direction to a child, but most often in the Old Testament, torah refers to the body of divine law.

Studying and delving into our faith is helpful, even if we aren't professional students. We can turn to respected sources for information, instruction or advice. Yet the best interpreter of the Word of God is the Spirit of God who emphasises and brings to our attention what we need to understand so as to better obey the Lord.

In a similar vein to our portion of Psalm 119, hymnwriter Frances Ridley Havergal prays that the Lord will speak to her, lead and feed her, strengthen her, give her rest, teach her, aid her words, fill her heart. The petitions aren't for her personal blessing but stem from a desire to pass the fullness of God on to others who need him, 'in living echoes' of his tone. We pray with her closing lines:

> O use me, Lord, use even me,
> Just as thou wilt and when and where,
> Until thy blessed face I see,
> Thy rest, thy joy, thy glory share.
>
> (*SASB* 612)

43

A Faith-Encouraging Promise

'The LORD will fight for you' (14:14).

The 'tipping point' plague is the death of Egypt's firstborn sons. On the night of their deliverance Israelite families are to slaughter a lamb and sprinkle its blood over the entry door-frames of their homes (12:21–23). The angel of death passes over the Israelites that eventful night, but Egypt's firstborn all perish, including the Pharaoh's son. Before morning the Pharaoh instructs Moses and his people to leave Egypt. He even asks them to bless him (vv. 31, 32). The Egyptians urge the Israelites to leave and give them articles of clothing, silver and gold.

Fearing he is losing the free labour of all these slaves, Pharaoh changes his mind. His army pursues and corners them by the Red Sea. The trapped Israelites complain bitterly to Moses that they would have been better off serving the Egyptians. Moses' faith-encouraging response is: 'Do not be afraid . . . The LORD will fight for you; you need only to be still' (14:13, 14).

In obedience to God's word Moses holds his staff out over the sea. With a strong east wind's assistance, dry land opens up through the water for them to escape to the other side. The wheels of the pursuing Egyptian chariots come off or become jammed in the muddy soil. At daybreak when Moses lifts his hand towards the sea, its waters flow back and engulf the Egyptian army. None survives.

The result? When they 'saw the great power the LORD displayed against the Egyptians, the people feared the LORD and put their trust in him and in Moses his servant' (v. 31). This deliverance becomes the great paradigm of salvation in the Old Testament that anticipates the greater deliverance secured by God through his Son, Jesus Christ, for the world. 'In Christ we have redemption through his blood, the forgiveness of sins' (Ephesians 1:7). Hallelujah!

To ponder:

'To him who loves us and has freed us from our sins by his blood, and has made us to be a kingdom and priests to serve his God and Father – to him be glory and power for ever and ever!' (Revelation 1:5, 6).

Let's Celebrate

'In your strength you will guide them to your holy dwelling' (v. 13).

Chapter 15 is the song of Moses and his sister Miriam celebrating Israel's remarkable redemption from the slavery of Egypt. Who gets the credit for this miraculous event? 'The LORD is my strength and my song; he has become my salvation' (v. 2). What kind of a God is able to do this? 'The Lord is a warrior . . . Your right hand, O LORD . . . majestic in holiness, awesome in glory' (vv. 3, 6, 11). The colourful imagery of verses 10 and 12 dramatises the extent of Yahweh's victory: 'You blew with your breath, and the sea covered them. They sank like lead in the mighty waters . . . You stretched out your right hand and the earth swallowed them.'

What about their future? God has a purpose for them corporately: 'In your unfailing love you will lead the people you have redeemed. In your strength you will guide them to your holy dwelling' (v. 13). Their neighbouring enemies in the Promised Land will not harm them. 'You will bring them in and plant them on the mountain of your inheritance . . . the sanctuary, O LORD, your hands established' (v. 17). They are to now live daily in the presence of their holy God. They can count on his unfailing love and divine strength to sustain them in their faith journey.

Israel's joyful celebration of God's rescuing them from the bondage of Egypt resonates well with Salvationists. Historically we have regarded joy as one of the hallmarks of Salvationism. Why? Because our being rescued from the guilt and grip of sin and from the curse of death through repentance and faith in Jesus Christ fills our hearts with heavenly joy. Like Israel, our enemies need not defeat us and we have been redeemed for a purpose – with God's strength and guidance we can live righteously in his holy presence.

> Joy floods my soul for Jesus has saved me,
> Freed me from sin that long had enslaved me,
> His precious blood he gave to redeem,
> Now I belong to him.
>
> *Norman John Clayton (SASB 349)*

What Does Holiness Look Like?

*'Don't suppose for a minute that I have come to demolish the Scriptures –
either God's Law or the Prophets. I'm not here to demolish but to complete.
I am going to put it all together' (Matthew 5:17, MSG).*

For Israel to be the holy people of God, a kingdom of priests, whose mission requires them to reflect the character of their God to the rest of the world, what would that individual and corporate holiness look like? Obedience to the Ten Commandments given to them at Mount Sinai will separate them in many ways from neighbouring nations and thus ensure their holiness before God. In this covenant relationship with God they can have no other gods, nor make any physical images of him. They must not 'misuse his name'. They are to especially honour God by keeping the seventh day of the week (Sabbath) 'holy'.

In human relationships they are to honour their parents, not murder, or commit adultery, steal, give false testimony about their neighbour or covet anything belonging to others. These are the foundation stones for a holy people. The ensuing chapters of Exodus (20:22–23:19) list many other laws to govern community living. Surely a sacred hush engulfs the people as Moses confirms the covenant by sprinkling the blood of a slain bull on the people, declaring: 'This is the blood of the covenant that the LORD has made with you in accordance with all these words' (24:8).

As a visible symbol of his presence with his people, God instructs Moses to build a tabernacle where he will be worshipped in a prescribed way (25:8–9). The majestic holiness of God requires that sin be dealt with; otherwise relationship with him is impossible. In the most sacred room of this holy place, the Holy of Holies, on the solemn Day of Atonement, the high priest will sprinkle the blood of a slain animal on the cover (mercy seat) of the ark of the covenant to atone for the people's sins. To be holy is to be cleansed from sin. The required death of the animal would ensure that Israel would never trivialise sin. The innocent died for the guilty, prefiguring the eventual perfect sacrifice by God's Son for the sins of the whole world.

Do We Need a Saviour?

'You know how prone these people are to evil' (v. 22).

When Moses later goes up Mount Sinai to receive instructions about the tabernacle, his people became impatient when he is gone for at least a week and begin to pressure Aaron, Moses' brother, to make for them gods they can see. Incredibly, Aaron acquiesces and, using their gold earrings and other metals, makes a calf. They even proclaim: 'These are your gods, O Israel, who brought you up out of Egypt' (v. 4). After such an awesome experience of God at Mount Sinai and freely entering into a solemn covenant with God, how can the Israelites so quickly disobey the first two commandments of the covenant? Because Moses represents God to them, do they now feel far from God because they can't see Moses? While he is on the mountain they create a substitute they can see.

Does this incident alert us to the danger of idolising certain Christian preachers and dynamic leaders so that when they move on, people lose interest in God and in living the Christian faith?

Aaron even builds an altar in front of the calf in preparation for a great festival the next day. God tells Moses he wants to destroy the Israelites for their blatant unfaithfulness. Moses passionately intercedes for his wayward people. Remembering the promise he made to them regarding their many descendants, God relents.

When Moses comes down from Sinai and sees the idolatrous celebration of his people he angrily throws down the two tablets with their Ten Commandments, breaking them to pieces. Aaron's pathetic explanation is: 'They gave me the gold, and I threw it into the fire, and out came this calf!' (v. 24). Do we recognise in this our own tendency to rationalise our sin?

Though tragic, this God-dishonouring event reveals the sacrificial heart of Moses: 'Please forgive their sin – but if not, blot me out of the book you have written' (v. 32). When Moses reflects on his impatience with his people and his sometimes impetuous actions, we see the spiritual growth in this servant of God. How have we grown in the grace of God?

Revealed but Hidden

'You will see my back; but my face must not be seen' (v. 23).

However self-confident the younger Moses was in killing the Egyptian who had been abusing Moses' fellow Hebrew, the trials of the ensuing years make him increasingly dependent upon God. In the idolatrous golden calf incident the abject failure of his people to worship only Yahweh rouses not only his anger towards his people but also his costly compassion for them.

In chapter 33 Moses grapples with the question, how can their holy God dwell with such a disloyal and sinful people? Does God still want to lead them into the land promised to their forefathers? Moses desperately wants God to teach him his ways so he can know that God is pleased with him. God reassures him: 'My Presence will go with you, and I will give you rest' (v. 14).

As we sometimes evaluate the options before us, do we feel, like Moses, the weighty responsibility of the calling to be part of the holy people of God (19:6)? Have we not found ourselves saying: 'What else will distinguish me and your people from all the other people on the face of the earth' (33:16)?

Have we ever felt so desperate for the assurance of God's presence that, like Moses, we have cried out from the depths of our being: 'Show me your glory' (v. 18)? Moses longs to experience the fullness of God's being or essence. God does reveal his glory. Moses discovers that, unlike the capricious gods of their neighbours, God's essential nature is goodness, mercy and compassion.

When the glory of God passes by him Moses discovers: 'You will see my back, but my face must not be seen' (v. 23). As a human, Moses will never fully experience the totality of God's being. Though knowable and accessible, God will remain inexhaustible and mysterious. Paradoxically, though revealed, God is also hidden – the kind of God we can never control. He is the only God worthy of our exclusive worship.

Grace that is Greater than All our Sin

'The glory of the LORD filled the tabernacle' (40:34).

God gives his rebellious people a second chance. He invites Moses to chisel out two new stone tablets on which he will write the words that were on the first tablets. He appears to Moses again on Mount Sinai, revealing himself as the 'compassionate and gracious God, slow to anger, abounding in love and faithfulness . . . forgiving . . . sin' (34:6, 7). Moses again begs God to forgive his people and to take them as his chosen ones. God renews the covenant relationship and gives the guidelines to be followed.

Having spoken with the Lord, Moses' face is radiant as he comes down the mountain. Time in God's holy presence in prayer, reading his Word and worshipping him will make us radiant too – radiant with his love, joy, peace and compassion. Moses gives the people the commands the Lord revealed to him (40:32). They are finally ready for the construction of the tabernacle (35:4–40:33), the visible symbol of God's holy and merciful presence with them.

When the tabernacle is finished there is an overwhelming sense of God's presence among the people (40:34). We sense the awe and mystery of God's holy presence in verses 36–37: 'In all the travels of the Israelites, whenever the cloud lifted from above the tabernacle, they would set out; but if the cloud did not lift, they did not set out – until the day it lifted.'

In the tabernacle the Holy One is dwelling among his people. Through its sacrificial system he provides graciously for their forgiveness. Yet after Israel's chronic covenant unfaithfulness God initiates a new covenant: 'The Word became flesh and made his dwelling among us. We have seen his glory . . . full of grace and truth' (John 1:14).

God also promised: 'I will give you a new heart . . . I will put my Spirit in you and move you to follow my decrees and . . . laws' (Ezekiel 36:26, 27). Eventually he not only tabernacles with his people; he tabernacles in them! 'When the Day of Pentecost came . . . all of them were filled with the Holy Spirit' (Acts 2:1, 4). Amen.

V – *Vau*

'I would walk in spaciousness, for I sought your commandments'
(v. 45, NETS).

In conjunction with United Nations Day (24 October), One World Week is observed in mid-October each year. The theme this year centres on peace. There are numerous ideas about the best way to promote world understanding.

Pope Paul VI said: 'If you want peace, work for justice.' Greg Mortenson, who followed through with a personal promise to help remote villages in Pakistan build schools (*Three Cups of Tea*), promotes concord through education. Many organisations, including The Salvation Army, engage in multifaceted assistance in immediate and long-range support of the needy worldwide.

The United Nations website challenges: 'What could you do to bring people together for a better understanding of different perspectives and to stimulate a positive change in the local and global community?'

Verse 45 of our psalm raises the question of different perspectives. The writer of Psalm 119 clearly values spaciousness, since in the verse the term he uses to signify freedom is literally 'a broad place'.

Whether we fear open spaces or thrive in them depends on whether we view open country as threatening or exhilarating. That perspective depends on our temperaments, the norms of our culture and environment as well as our own experiences. Some children of the city fear open spaces. Others who have always known open spaces fear the noise and activity of a city.

For the psalmist, open space equates with self-determination of spirit. He attributes enjoying such prized liberty of spirit to his continuous pursuit of God's truth and wisdom. What a wonderful paradox – binding ourselves to the Word brings freedom. Or as hymnwriter George Matheson pens:

'Make me a captive, Lord, and then I shall be free'
(*SASB* 508).

Suffering's Iridescence

Personal suffering may seem as pointless as unjust treatment at the whim of a powerful tyrant. Although primarily affecting one part of our being, chronic illness, disability and other kinds of affliction threaten a shortfall of wholeness in other areas. We are integrated beings, and one part influences the others. If we are deficient in one area it doesn't mean we have to succumb to hopelessness in all areas – our body, emotions, intellect and spirit. We are more than the sum of our scars.

Creative ways of triumphing over adversity inspire and encourage us. Often through relating their stories, those who live with suffering can offer lessons for others who also live in chaos, for loved ones who live with the chaos, and for those who, although not directly affected, nevertheless care about those who suffer in our world. God, the best storyteller, includes some of the stories in Scripture. We identify with Jacob who wrestled with the angel and lived with his limp. We're interested in Paul's 'thorn in the flesh'. Even in the age of Facebook and texting, storytelling has its place.

As we look into a few of the questions surrounding suffering, we sometimes find what at first seems to be an unlikely stance – that although not heaven-sent, trials can be heaven-blessed; that a fine pearl's iridescent surface surrounds its unsought irritant.

In *The Praying Life*, Deborah Douglas reminds us that today we want relief from suffering, as the solution to our problems. Christians of earlier centuries, without as many means of aid, focused instead on Christ's companionship with them in suffering and their radical healing in life after death. She writes:

> If we surrender our own limited vision of what our healing might be, if we can accept that presence is worth more than 'recovery', we may be amazed at what God has in mind for us. This may not be 'healing' as the world sees it. But to bear such unhealed wounds with courage and trust and generosity of spirit is to live close to the heart of God and to live toward the promised day of resurrection.[8]

Choose Joy

*'I gave up all that inferior stuff so I could know Christ personally,
experience his resurrection power, be a partner in his suffering,
and go all the way with him to death itself' (v. 10, MSG).*

In the Old Testament, affliction meant either denying or humbling oneself
or being humbled or deprived by someone or something else. Besides
difficulties inherent to the human condition since the beginning, God's
judgement for intentional sin and the forces of evil which sought to thwart
God's purposes were also seen as sources of affliction.

In the New Testament, affliction is sometimes 'suffering'. It too is seen
as coming in general to all or as the result of an individual's sin, but can
also be persecution as a result of faithfulness to Christ or as a discipline to
help a believer mature.

Today we probably think of suffering as a personal matter, even if it
comes to us indirectly. However we view it, when it affects us we want to
make sense of it. If there's an illness, we want a name for it and the hope
of some relief from its effects. If there is no relief, we at least want to learn
how to cope. It reassures us to know that God knows our situation and that
even lengthy suffering is not the whole story. For the believer, there will
ultimately be more than release; there will be triumph and wholeness.

At times God delivers us from suffering, but if he doesn't, he can use
suffering for his eternal purposes. Jesus' example encourages us to be
faithful, to use the gift of prayer, to take opportunities to empathise with
and comfort others who suffer, to persevere.

Will You Choose Joy? is a book compiled from sermon notes on
Philippians. It comes alive because the writer, Normajean Honsberger,
delivered those sermons near the end of her four decades of life, after her
husband's death and in the midst of her own ordeal with cancer, treatments
and their effects. She said, 'God doesn't ask of me something he hasn't
empowered me to do . . . I can't change my circumstances. The only
control I have is how I respond to them. I choose joy!'[9]

Choose Utility

*'I just let Christ take over! And so the weaker I get,
the stronger I become' (v. 10, MSG).*

She didn't want to be there. Besides being uncomfortable and inconvenient, last year's tests weren't conclusive and meant she had to return for an in-depth follow-up. So she prayed for courage, arrived at the office on time and with the requisite information. Just before she walked through the door she asked the Lord to help her to be a blessing to someone else. The receptionist smiled cheerily. The wait was brief, the first technician pleasant and helpful, the test bearable.

As she waited between tests, a busy nurse who saw her with her diary paused to ask if she was getting organised. In fact the woman was praying for people listed on her prayer pages and said so. The nurse's focused professional front melted: 'I could use your prayers too,' she implored. The young nurse had a son with disabilities and found coping with his needs and her own work both tiring and trying. Patty's name was on the prayer page before the woman moved to the next X-ray room.

On occasion Charles Wesley considered debilitating illness an opportunity. When he was set aside he could afford time to write hymns. Many of his hymns, like David's psalms, come out of difficult times and connect with others who suffer. When he ties personal suffering with what God is willing to bear, words of hope emerge. His influence continues as we still sing many of the hymns he wrote. Some of the less well-known especially point us to God's faithfulness to his people in distress, such as the one which begins: 'And are we yet alive?' (*SASB* 915)

God is with us in our suffering, but does not seek to prolong it. Over time Charles Wesley, who lived with chronic physical ailments and their accompanying dejection for most of his eighty years, dealt with pain and mental distress by allowing the power of Scripture to assure his spirit, and by cultivating the support of friends in the faith. That eighteenth-century prescription still works.

Choose Endurance

'God is educating you; that's why you must never drop out . . .
This trouble you're in isn't punishment; it's training' (v. 7, MSG).

The French proverb, *On va bien loin dépuis qu'on est las*, is true: 'One can go a long way after one is weary.' Among other endeavours, sport and exploration give evidence of the difference endurance can make to seemingly unattainable progress.

Endurance combined with certainty yields tenacity. As believers we are not called to passively hang on, but to move ahead with whatever God directs us to do – whether the effort involves visible action or interaction, or invisible attitudes or prayer.

In Revelation 3:10, when Christ encourages the church in Philadelphia: 'Because you kept my Word in passionate patience, I'll keep you safe in the time of testing that will be here soon', he commends their patient, steadfast waiting for him and continues with the assurance: 'I'm on my way; I'll be there soon. Keep a tight grip on what you have so no one distracts you and steals your crown' (v. 11, *MSG*).

In each of the seven epistles to churches that Jesus dictates to John in Revelation, he promises to give rewards to those who 'overcome'. John uses the verb for 'overcome' without an object. Overcome what, we ask? Besides a general injunction to stay true to the Lord and his purposes in our lives, perhaps in part it also applies to us individually. As believers we may deduce what we need to overcome by listening to what the Spirit says to us regarding our personal challenges and our everyday lives.

Someone has said, 'We rise by the things that are under our feet.' The motto of nineteenth-century Scottish publisher and author Robert Chambers is said to have been: 'He that tholes [old Scottish word for 'bears' or 'puts up with'], overcomes.'

To ponder:

'Patient endurance attaineth to all things; who God possesseth in nothing is wanting; alone God sufficeth.'

Teresa of Avila (*SASB* 956)

Choose Hope

'I pray that God, the source of hope, will fill you completely with joy and peace because you trust in him. Then you will overflow with confident hope through the power of the Holy Spirit' (Romans 15:13, NLT).

In his prayer at the dedication of the first temple, Solomon addressed the Lord as one who keeps his covenant of love with those who live in sincere obedience to him. The king asked that when unsought calamity of any kind came, the Lord would hear the prayers of any who prayed with transparent, honest hearts and that he would forgive and act accordingly. Then they would live in grateful, worshipful obedience to the Lord.

When we know God's forgiveness, we want to live to please him. So we understand the psalmist's testimony: 'Before I was afflicted I went astray, but now I obey your word' (Psalm 119:67). We're glad for the corrective of the word for our hearts. We well know that behaviour often leads to predictable consequences. Abuse the body and expect some malfunction.

But what about those who lead health-conscious lives and are stricken with diseases usually associated with neglect or excess, or those who find themselves in unexpected unmanageable predicaments? Sometimes there is no apparent reason for affliction.

Solomon's request reflects the Old Testament mindset that trouble comes as a result of sin. Sometimes it does, but at other times trouble just comes. Jesus corrected the Old Testament view (John 9). Even when troubles don't stem from sin, they too can drive us to God. Struggles which compel us to live by grace may bring us a sense of the nearness of God unknown at carefree times.

Dr David Ireland, a pastor in New Jersey, USA, encouraged those who had done all they could to seek human and divine help yet continued to struggle with unrelenting, unrelieved difficulties. His sermon from the life of Joseph illustrated the best outlook for believers cornered by unwelcome circumstances: 'I'm here by God's appointment, in his keeping, under his training and for his timing.' I plan to remember that hopeful reminder.

Choose Christ's Course

*'Because of the joy awaiting him, he endured the Cross,
disregarding its shame' (Hebrews 12:2, NLT).*

Leslie D. Weatherhead was a British theologian and minister of City
Temple in London for twenty-four years. After the Second World War
he raised funds to rebuild the church which had been gutted by fire bombs.
He wrote *A Private House of Prayer* while at City Temple. I received a well-
read copy from a British Salvation Army officer missionary couple who
lived Weatherhead's prayer as they bravely yet privately coped with
suffering.

> Let me not suppose, O God, that every pain and disease and disability
> is thy will or man's fault. Disease and pain are never thy desire for men,
> and everywhere the Saviour went, he delivered men and in that
> deliverance did thy will.
>
> Some things may be my fault, my ignorance, my folly, my sin, my
> worry and fear and lack of faith. But some are my share of the evil of
> the world. I receive good that I have not merited. It comes from the
> goodness, the wisdom, the skill of others. Sometimes I must bear the
> disabilities that come from belonging to the human family. And Satan is
> at work seeking to spoil thy lovely world.
>
> Whatever the cause of my ill, help me to vanquish it and to feel that
> thou art in partnership with me trying to conquer it, and if it may not
> yet be utterly defeated, teach me that thou wilt never let it claim a
> victory. Thou wilt weave it into thy plan and make it serve thy purposes
> which are wholly loving and wise, and ultimately omnipotent.
>
> In the meantime, dear Lord, make me cheerful and patient, coming
> to terms with any suffering which I am called upon to bear, and let thy
> joy at the bottom of my heart bubble up into consciousness, so that my
> witness may be brave and that I do not do a disservice to thy cause by
> downcast moods and tearful eyes. Amen.[10]

Choose Disproportionate Gain

*'These little troubles (which are really so transitory) are winning
for us a permanent, glorious and solid reward out of all proportion
to our pain' (v. 17, JBP).*

This passage from 2 Corinthians shows a number of contrasts: outwardly wasting away yet inwardly renewed (v. 16); present and future (v. 17); visible but temporary; eternal yet unseen (v. 18); earthly and heavenly (5:1).

In our key verse Paul acknowledges our present hardships to be afflictions and stressful by nature, yet in the context of eternity, not as weighty or long-lived as they currently seem. 'Afflictions which befall Christians assume a supernatural significance. They are never merely accidental; they are divinely permitted with a purpose, and overruled to our eternal good, if we bear them devoutly.'[11]

Paul calls our current afflictions 'light'. If he hadn't experienced so many hardships, we would wonder if he knew what he was talking about. But he isn't a stoic. He knows discouragement. When he occasionally delineates what he's faced (11:23–29), he isn't flippant.

It's interesting that the Greek word used for light here, which means lightweight or easy to bear, is used in only one other place in the New Testament – when Jesus says, 'My yoke is easy and my burden is light' (Matthew 11:30). It's the burden allowed by and shared by Christ which becomes bearable.

Paul also says our afflictions are brief, momentary. We may accept that outlook, yet may find it difficult to realise in the midst of seemingly endless sorrow, chronic illness, relentless pain, disability, weariness, separation, fear, loss or the unknown.

Current afflictions can also be counted light compared with the graces they're accomplishing in us now as well as with what we'll see they've accomplished for us when there's a full disclosure – a disproportionately, exceptionally weighty reward. We need to redirect the focus of our telescope from our situation to our destination. The suffering will end and God in Christ will make us complete, unshakeable and victorious forever (1 Peter 5:10).

Z – Zain

'Your statutes were musical tunes to me in my place of sojourn'
(v. 54, NETS).

We ended last Sunday's comments with the delightful paradox found in the freedom of being Christ's captives, slaves, servants. New Testament writers refer to evangelists of the gospel as bond-servants of Christ. Paul says that Jesus took the form of a slave for us (Philippians 2:7). On the eve of his crucifixion Jesus reminded his disciples to follow his example, declaring that he was among them as one who served (Luke 22:27).

As the psalmist begins today's octuplet he asks the Lord to remember his word to his servant, as he describes himself. He points to promises that God has given him which provide hope and comfort in time of trouble.

The promises from God's Word that come to us during difficulty strengthen and encourage us. Our need etches them on our hearts in ways that problem-free days don't. When the trouble has passed, we can benefit from reviewing such promises and noticing their patterns.

The promises God gives his followers sustain us wherever we are – even if away from our literal or figurative homelands or comfort zones, or perhaps especially when away from them. The psalmist says that God's word is the theme of his song in his sojourn on earth (v. 54). As the exile sings songs of home, so we sing songs of our eternal home – heaven.

Reflecting not just on the promises, but also on who gives them, can aid us during wakefulness during the dark, moonless nights of illness, loneliness, worry or fear. Such reflections during the long nights may in turn become a blessing to others. Hymnwriter Fanny Crosby recalled: 'Most of my poems have been written during the long night watches.'

Best of all, Jesus comes to us as he did to his frightened disciples and brings the strengthening words: 'It is I. Don't be afraid' (Matthew 14:27).

As Things Change

*'He comforts us in all our troubles so that we can comfort others . . . We will
be able to give them the same comfort God has given us' (v. 4, NLT).*

In *Being Well When We're Ill*,[12] theologian, writer and educator, Marva
Dawn, who herself faces multiple disabilities, talks about how comforting
it is to realise that as Christians our suffering can have significance and
influence well beyond our immediate circumstances or even our times.

It helps to remember that we are part of a wider circle of believers who
grapple with unwanted physical hindrances; that there can be meaning in
the midst of pain; that God is with us and offers us hope and wholeness.
Through the difficulties we face and the way we view and handle them, we
may gain unique insights. The Lord may be preparing us to share such
discoveries with others who can benefit from the principles and apply
them to their own unique circumstances.

In an interview with *Christianity Today* about what spiritual lessons he
was learning, Tony Snow – US White House press secretary, husband and
father of three who subsequently died in 2008 at age fifty-one – said: 'You
discover that Christianity is not something doughy, passive, pious, and
soft. The life of belief teems with thrills, boldness, danger, shocks, reversals,
triumphs and epiphanies.'

In an article subtitled 'When you enter the valley of the shadow of death
things change',[13] he shared some realisations which came during his
struggle with cancer: maladies remind us of our mortality, but Scripture
offers us salvation and God's grace; believers are born into life, not death
and the journey continues; challenges strengthen our faith and present
opportunities for unparalleled wisdom and joy; we can follow Jesus'
example when facing the cross and let love change everything.

> Sorrow hides beneath her wings
> Recompense for sufferings,
> And the blessing waits for us
> In the garden near the cross.
> *Albert Orsborn* (*SASB* 145)

Out of Extremity

'We don't yet see things clearly. We're squinting in a fog, peering through a mist. But it won't be long before the weather clears and the sun shines bright! We'll see it all then, see it all as clearly as God sees us, knowing him directly just as he knows us!' (v. 12, MSG)

Suffering and loss have in their disruption of the status quo spurred some on to become inventors, political leaders, entrepreneurs, preachers, artists. Generally it's long after their contributions, when we look back through the lens of history, that we realise the role hardship played.

When something is broken, hidden creativity can spring up and find alternative expressions. As difficult and unwelcome as suffering is, some of the creative ways people have found to cope with its many aspects uplift and encourage us in our struggles.

Prominent writers who have battled illness often reveal that focusing on something outside of themselves helped them. Writer Susan Vreeland surrounded herself with beauty in preparation for lymphoma treatments. She wrote her first book, *Girl in Hyacinth Blue*, while coping with treatments, isolation and recovery. Recognising that art can emerge out of extremity, she also discovered that: 'Creative endeavour can aid healing because it lifts us out of self-absorption and gives us a goal.'

Cartoonist Roy Mitchell, creator of *The Chalks and Cheeses* and the *God is . . .* collection, found strength in his relationship with God while battling cancer. In 2009, through his book, *God is . . .* , and his visits to churches, he focused on telling people about God's love. He said: 'Cancer makes you realise what the really important things are in life. And the most important thing to me is being close to God. So now I want to be an encouragement to people.'

Whether applied to a difficult assignment in a distant land or an unwelcome illness or dilemma, 'coming out stronger' seems like a platitude until afterwards when it can be fully realised. Some will know a measure of that gratification. Christians can live in hope and trust God for the wide-angle view, even if not seen until later.

To Christ

*'[Even] now I rejoice in the midst of my sufferings on your behalf.
And in my own person I am making up whatever is still lacking and
remains to be completed [on our part] of Christ's afflictions,
for the sake of His body, which is the Church' (v. 24, AB).*

The question of suffering baffles us. Even if we can get past asking 'why?' in our personal context, we still wonder about the role suffering plays in the world. Perhaps beyond the 'why?' we should ask 'where?' and 'how?' Where can I see God at work in the midst of suffering? How is God not only helping me, but making me a blessing? In *The Wounded Healer*, Henri Nouwen speaks of the possibility of God using our wounds to help others.

When William Booth wrote of Christ's command to all Christians to go into the world, he used the term 'suffering to Christ' to explain that going would entail suffering not only for the cause of Christ but in serving others as if they were Christ himself. Major Andrew Miller further states: 'Suffering was an intrinsic aspect of the identity of Salvationists. "Suffering to Christ" is a theme that encapsulates William Booth's ecclesiology in a unique and powerful way.'[14]

In the early 1900s Booth's son, Bramwell, wrote: 'Is it possible that the sorrow and suffering which fall upon those who are entirely surrendered to God and his work are, in some hidden way, sorrow and suffering for others?'[15]

In Colossians 1:24, when Paul says he participates in Christ's afflictions, it's not for the redemption of the world but for building up the Church. In that vein Marva Dawn says: 'We never know how what we are going through can be beneficial for others or an offering to God, but it is. Even more, God takes everything – all that we are and experience – and knits it to Christ's Cross.'[12]

In that light, we see that whatever we or someone we love suffers today, in the end, holds meaning.

A Harmony of Healing and Wholeness

'The prayer of a person living right with God is something
powerful to be reckoned with' (v. 16, MSG).

James advises his readers that just as we should praise God in times of joy, we should pray in times of trouble and ask for others' prayers as well when we're ill. He refers to the double blessing of spiritual healing. Jesus did so as well when he commanded the people he both healed and forgave to go and 'sin no more'.

Sin and illness are not inextricably linked, but when there is unconfessed sin, that disease needs to be purged.

In her notes for a six-part study titled *Sickness, Suffering and Healing*, Mrs Commissioner Flora Larsson wrote:

> The Army Founder, William Booth, took a definite stand on the belief that God could heal the sick in answer to faith and prayer. He wrote in *The War Cry*: 'This is in perfect harmony with the views and experience of The Salvation Army from the beginning. Nothing to the contrary has ever been taught by our authority, and numerous instances of faith-healing have occurred in the Army throughout its history.'

Flora Larsson reminds us that just as the spiritual atmosphere of Christian meetings can be warmed by songs, prayers and testimonies which encourage faith, our own outlook can be helped by the things we read, hear, watch and talk about that aid our peace in trusting the Lord. Doctors and medicine complement prayer and faith.

Yet some are not healed. We don't know why. We do know that God loves us whether we are healed or not. We've been told that 'every Salvationist has the privilege and responsibility of involvement in health, healing and wholeness'.[16]

Perhaps you ask yourself, as I do: 'In what ways do I, not a caregiver or professional health worker, participate?'

Live the Cry

*'Strengthen yourselves in the Lord and in the power which his
supreme might imparts' (v. 10, WNT).*

As we think about ways to contribute to 'health, healing and wholeness'
our role can start nearby with people whose needs we know. The
psalmists cried out to God for deliverance while holding tightly to his
faithfulness, and we can too. We pray for those who suffer, and look for
practical, thoughtful ways to encourage them.

Do we have a particular pain that can stimulate us to pray for others in
similar or greater straits? Does considering our blessings, however modest,
prompt us to pray for those who lack even the basics of clean water,
wholesome food and a safe place to live?

Millions lack essential medical aid and some systems in the world
perpetuate the poverty in which those millions live. We pray for those who
suffer and against the forces of evil that inflict injustice. We pray for
wisdom and caring for those with the power and resources to make a
difference.

At the conclusion of his letter to the Ephesians, Paul calls his readers to
be strong in God and God's power by wearing and using the armour God
provides to counteract the unseen but powerful forces of evil in our world.
Moreover, Paul urges: 'And pray in the Spirit on all occasions with all kinds
of prayers and requests. With this in mind, be alert and always keep on
praying for all the saints' (v. 18).

God will help his followers to see ways to counter the injustices of evil
through our votes, our support of organisations that offer hope and help,
our articulation of a desire for change. Some will contribute financially or
through thoughtful purchases which aid agencies of healing and hope.
Some may become aware of a divine call to go to a place of need, while
others may be called to enable and support their going.

> Across the street or around the world,
> the mission's still the same,
> proclaim and live the truth
> in Jesus' name.
> *Jon Mohr and Randall Dennis*[17]

Survival Arts

'Find someone who plays well and bring him to me' (v. 17).

As commented on Tuesday, the arts have brought meaning, survival, healing and hope to people in harsh, impossible situations. Long ago King Saul's advisers recommended music to help lift his melancholy.

The film *Paradise Road* tells the story of women prisoners of war in the Pacific who used music to relieve their misery. In Venezuela, music has been the antidote to street violence, offering dignity, purpose and safety to many families.

In 1899 Jean Sibelius wrote the symphonic poem *Finlandia* as part of a covert protest against increasing censorship from Russia. The stirring sections evoke the Finish national struggle. But the symphony closes on a calmer note in the serene *Finlandia Hymn*.

The hymn we sing to it, 'Be still, my soul', encourages us to bear trouble patiently, leave the unfolding and providing to God and trust that in his faithfulness, although through trials, he will lead us to final joy. We can understand why it was athlete, missionary and prisoner-of-war Eric Liddell's favourite.

Art therapists treat various disabilities through encouraging artistic expression of many kinds. Just so, as part of an innovative United Nations project, artist Ross Bleckner helped former child soldiers in Uganda come to terms with their experiences.

William Williams, the eighteenth-century Welsh minister and writer of more than 1,000 hymns (including 'Guide me, O Thou Great Jehovah'), was said to have sung all Wales into religion. Early-day Salvationist Elwin Oliphant said that Williams lived in times of social upheaval but instead of despairing preached salvation and instead of rousing sang his country into faith.[18]

There are endless possibilities for colour, harmony, drama, poetry and other facets of the creative arts to ease pain of body, mind or spirit and bring delight and hope. When we consider that our creativity reflects our Creator's, we will want to ask the Holy Spirit to awaken us to ways he wants to use it to relieve suffering.

Ch – *Cheth*

'Teach me thine orders, for the world is full of thy goodness' (v. 64, JMT).

At the market, if we want to buy the best fruit or vegetables we turn produce over and inspect it carefully. At a stall selling embroidered pieces, we check the back of the work to see how closely the reverse side resembles the front. In a similar careful way, the psalmist says he inspects his own conduct.

When he sees that his ways don't line up with God's he doesn't launch a self-improvement regimen or seek out others for mutual pity. He knows where to turn. He turns to God's word (v. 59).

Verses 57–60 seem to be a unit. He begins with a summary declaration – he has found God to be his portion, his inheritance (v. 57). Not only does the psalmist turn to God's word when he recognises his need; he seeks God with his whole heart, trusting God to treat him as he's promised, with grace and mercy (v. 58). He resolves to hurry to obey what God says without delay (v. 60). He gives notice that he promises to obey the Lord (v. 57).

He is determined to stay the course in spite of what those who oppose God may do to him. He is committed to God, even thanking him for his word in the middle of the night. He feels one with all who worship God and live according to his word.

Throughout the centuries there have been countless examples of believers who have echoed the psalmist's determination, and faithfully followed through, often at great cost. Most of them are unknown. We thank God for those we have encountered. Their lives encourage us to adhere closely to God and his word. We will think of them tomorrow when some churches celebrate All Saints Day.

Various names are prominent in church history. It was 493 years ago today that Martin Luther posted his reasoned Ninety-Five Theses on the church door in Wittenberg, Germany. This year Reformation Sunday and Reformation Day coincide.

———————

To pray:

Lord, we thank you for your Word and all the pioneers and veterans of the faith who have wrapped their lives around it. Help us to cling to it and follow you in spirit and in truth.

Sojourner Jacob
Genesis 28–50

Introduction

The second half of Genesis presents a cast of opposites: Isaac and Rebekah, Jacob and Esau, Rachel and Leah, and Jacob's sons.

Isaac and Rebekah are opposites who attract. When the couple have twin boys who also display opposite temperaments, Isaac's favourite is the one who behaves like his wife, and Rebekah's favourite is the one like her husband (Genesis 25:28). Tensions in the family mount and the brothers part on less-than-friendly terms, not to meet again for twenty years.

We follow the life of Jacob; note his developing faith; see God's covenant continuing through him; watch him worship; and observe God's provision through upright Joseph.

Last autumn an atheist campaign in New York City posted large advertisements in underground stations: 'A million New Yorkers are good without God. Are you?' Jacob's life paints a bold answer, 'NO, NEVER!' By the close of Jacob's journeys, dreams, disappointments and restored hopes he is certain God has been his lifelong shepherd and angel of deliverance.

Teresa of Avila's words would have resonated with Jacob and can with us as well:

> Let nothing disturb thee,
> Nothing affright thee;
> All things are passing,
> God never changeth!
> Patient endurance attaineth to all things;
> Who God possesseth in nothing is wanting;
> Alone God sufficeth.
> > (*SASB* 956) trs. Henry Wadsworth Longfellow

Setting the Stage

'May God Almighty bless you and make you fruitful and increase your numbers until you become a community of peoples' (v. 3).

We resume the Genesis saga (from September 2009) after Sarah has died and Isaac, son of Abraham and son of promise, has married Rebekah of Mesopotamia. When Abraham dies, his sons Ishmael and Isaac, one-time rivals, bury him in the cave where Sarah was buried.

As with Abraham and Sarah, Isaac and Rebekah wait a long time for children to be born – twenty years, until Isaac is sixty. When Rebekah asks the Lord why she feels such jostling in her womb, he tells her that she'll have twins; two unequal nations will come from them; the older will serve the younger.

Isaac and Rebekah name their boys based on their impressions of them at birth – Esau (hairy) and Jacob (heel-catcher). Esau, like his father's half-brother, Ishmael, becomes a skilled hunter of wild animals whereas Jacob is quiet, as his father had been, and stays near home, caring for domesticated animals and learning to cook. Surprisingly, the younger one, Jacob, is the son of promise.

Esau unwisely forfeits his birthright for a bowl of Jacob's stew. Like his father, Esau marries at forty. Later, when Isaac is 137 and wants to give Esau a blessing before he dies, Esau misses out again, this time through his mother and brother's deception. No wonder he plans to murder Jacob as soon as Isaac dies.

Rebekah intervenes again. On the premise that she wants Jacob to marry someone from her people, instead of from an idolatrous people as Esau has done, she asks Isaac to send Jacob back to her homeland. Esau's Canaanite wives had brought Isaac and Rebekah grief. She touches a soft-spot and Isaac agrees. The stage is set. Jacob, who is off to find a wife, will discover much more.

In retrospect, this is part of God's overall plan to include Jacob in the chain of his purposes and covenant. It would have been better for everyone if Isaac, Rebekah, Jacob and Esau had cooperated with God's plan. But they continue to learn that in spite of their sidetracks, God reigns. He still does.

Guaranteed Return Trip

*'I am with you and will watch over you wherever you go, and I
will bring you back to this land. I will not leave you until I have
done what I have promised you' (v. 15).*

Jacob cooperates with his mother again. This time it's for protection
from his angry brother. Once Isaac releases Jacob with his blessing, the
homebody sets off on an adventure that will take him hundreds of miles
from home for many years. As Rebekah sends him off to her brother, she
may encourage him with her own recollection of leaving home years before
and travelling to an unknown land to marry Isaac, sight unseen.

Rebekah assures her favourite son that she will send for him when the
situation improves. Jacob may think his ageing father will die before he
returns, but he has no way of knowing he will never see his mother alive
again.

We wonder how Jacob feels as he walks further and further away from
everything familiar. Does his aloneness become loneliness? He has time for
reflection. When there's no more daylight, he stops for the night. He
chooses a stone for a pillow; we hope it's a smooth one. Considering his
exertion and circumstances, we may not be surprised that he sleeps and
dreams, yet the nature of the dream is remarkable. He sees a stairway to
heaven with angels going up and down. He hears the Lord identifying
himself as the God of his father and grandfather, and then promising that
the covenant blessing would continue through Jacob.

When he left home, his father prayed for Jacob's safe return to and
prosperity in their land. The Lord promises that too, but adds that he will
be with him and watch over him in the interim. The lonely figure must be
greatly encouraged to discover that he is not abandoned. His morning
worship includes recognising that the place and the stone are uncommon,
not in themselves, but because he's met God there. He calls the place
'House of God' and vows that since (not if) God is with him to provide for
him, keep him and bring him back home, then he is Jacob's God. He is ours
too.

A New Life Unfolds

'Rachel came with her father's sheep, for she was a shepherdess' (v. 9).

Jacob's overnight encounter with God encourages him and in the morning he sets off confidently, possibly eagerly. The Hebrew text says he 'lifted up his feet'. Perhaps he runs part of the way. We aren't told how long it takes Jacob to reach his destination or any other details of his journey, but in a day without sophisticated navigational devices or even detailed maps, the trip on his own and safe arrival in Paddan Aram are notable.

When he reaches the vicinity, it must be heartening for Jacob, himself a shepherd, to see flocks and shepherds even if their actions puzzle him. Why would they be waiting around the well and not watering their animals? He doesn't know the customs of the area. When Jacob learns that the shepherds know his uncle and that Laban's shepherdess daughter, Rachel, is bringing a flock to the well, he must be amazed and convinced of God's providence.

Yet in his resourcefulness, Jacob, who wants to move the shepherds out of the picture, tells them not to waste the day, but water their sheep and get back to the pastures. They'll not have it. The well's heavy stone cover comes off only when all the flocks are present. This practice could be to keep the water clean or from evaporating, to assure that all share equally, to respect the owner's rights of oversight or because the stone's weight requires united effort.

Jacob sees Rachel and is smitten. If he can't dismiss the other men, he can at least show off his strength. Before he introduces himself, he removes the heavy stone cover on his own, and then waters Rachel's flock. That gesture and an emotional disclosure of who he is touch Rachel who runs for her father. Jacob is welcome.

Laban may recall that decades earlier his sister, Rebekah, also ran home with news of a stranger's arrival. But this time we don't hear the traveller giving God due credit for guidance as Abraham's servant did. When we see God's hand at work in our lives, when things work out better than we could have imagined, do we openly praise God?

Jacob's Household

'But grow in the grace and knowledge of our Lord and Saviour Jesus Christ'
(2 Peter 3:18).

By the time Jacob recounts his journey and his family history, Laban is convinced Jacob is his sister's son. Jacob makes himself useful, so his uncle offers to pay him. Jacob, who loves Rachel, quickly offers to work for his uncle for seven years if he can marry Rachel. They agree on the proposal, which suits both of them.

The enamoured Jacob sees his beloved every day and seven years pass quickly. Laban arranges the wedding feast. But the father switches his daughters and gives Jacob Leah, Rachel's older sister, instead. The next morning reveals what the veil of darkness hid. The one called supplanter has been tricked and feels ill-used.

His uncle's matter-of-fact explanation that it's customary for the eldest daughter to marry first doesn't change Jacob's sense of being unfairly treated. Laban offers to give Rachel to Jacob in exchange for seven more years of work. This time Jacob can have his bride in advance. Laban also gives each of his daughters a personal maid.

Since Jacob loves Rachel and not Leah, the elder is not in an ideal position. The sisters do not share Jacob equally, yet the Lord is aware that Leah is not loved and blesses her with conception.

In a culture where motherhood equates with womanhood and having many children is a wife's highest ambition, although not Jacob's chosen one, Leah's fertile son-producing womb brings her value in others' eyes and some self-esteem. Their first son is Reuben ('Look, a son') and causes her to rejoice in God's mercy to her. The Lord has seen her misery (v. 32). She names their next son Simeon ('One who hears') because she's certain the Lord has heard of her unloved status (v. 33). At the birth of Levi ('Attached') she hopes for Jacob's attachment (v. 34). She names their fourth son Judah ('Praise') and wisely says: 'This time I will praise the LORD' (v. 35). Besides the joy of new life entering Jacob's family, significantly, some of the members show seedlings of faith in his God.

God's Increase

'Children are a gift from the LORD; they are a reward from him'
(Psalm 127:3, NLT).

Jacob has a full household of two wives, their maids and four sons. But Rachel finds it a lopsided one and her envy of her sister for having children becomes desperation. She demands that Jacob give her children. When he lashes out in anger and frustration: 'Am I God?' he acknowledges in an indirect way that things of divine prerogative are beyond his control.

Rachel resorts to taking things into her own hands and, in a tactic Sarah used with Abraham, decides she will have children through a surrogate mother, her maid. Bilhah bears a boy and Rachel names him Dan ('Vindication'), declaring that in mercy God has taken her side. The maid has another son whom Rachel names Naphtali ('Wrestling' or 'Entwining'), as Rachel sees her struggle with Leah.

Not to be outdone in the baby competition, when Leah stops having children, she offers Jacob her maid as another surrogate mother. Zilpah bears two sons. Leah calls them Gad ('Good fortune' or 'Reward') and Asher ('Happy' or 'Blessed'). Leah isn't finished. She and Jacob have Issachar ('Reward') and Zebulun ('Honour'). Although still looking for Jacob's favour, increasingly Leah gives God credit for her sons (v. 20). She also presents Jacob with a daughter, Dinah.

Jacob has eleven children. Finally, after Rachel's humiliation of years of barrenness, her prayers are answered and she becomes pregnant. Jacob's mother and grandmother, themselves barren for years, could have empathised with Rachel's state of mind when her son is born and she says: 'God has taken away my disgrace'. She names him Joseph ('Addition') and hopes that having a son will signal God's further mercy and she'll have another (v. 24).

Waiting is difficult, especially when we would rather do something about the desired outcome. Eventually both sisters come to acknowledge that, ultimately, God is in control of increase. We should acknowledge that too.

The Farewell

'May the LORD keep watch between us to make sure that we keep this covenant when we are out of each other's sight' (v. 49, NLT).

The birth of Joseph, Rachel's firstborn, may be a turning point since Jacob subsequently plans to leave Paddan Aram. His father-in-law counters Jacob's proposal and asks him to stay and even name his price. The offer sounds familiar. Jacob is ready. He'll stay for a little longer if he can have all the less-sought-after animals of the flocks – those with spotted, speckled or black coats. Laban agrees and promptly separates the identifiable animals from the apparent pure-breds so they don't cross-breed and benefit Jacob.

For the next six years, in spite of Laban's deteriorating attitude, frequent changes to the contract and unfair practices with Jacob's wages, Jacob doesn't neglect his work. God takes care of Jacob's interests and prepares him to become a people. When in a dream 'the God of Bethel' directs Jacob to return home, he privately tells Rachel and Leah of his plans to leave. They heartily agree that their father has ill-used all of them and that if God says to leave, they should do it.

By the time Laban hears that they've left him and pursues their convoy of people and flocks, their course is set and he can't dissuade them. Surprisingly, he too receives a word from God in a dream, a warning not to prevent Jacob's journey (v. 29).

In a similar vein as when Laban and his father released Rebekah to travel with Eliezer to meet and marry Abraham's son (Genesis 24:50), Laban says that God has warned him not to argue with Jacob about leaving, since it is of the Lord.

So they come to yet another agreement, the best one yet, and covenant to do no harm to each other. They set up a pile of stones and call it Mizpah (watchtower). Laban vows in the name of the God of their honoured, but long-deceased, ancestors while Jacob exercises a more current faith as he vows by the one he calls 'the Fear of his father', the one he first personally encountered at Bethel on the journey out and whom he is learning to trust.

T – *Teth*

'Be good to your servant, GOD; be as good as your Word' (v. 65, MSG).

The simple word 'good' appears repeatedly in this section. Think of some of its synonyms: favourable, bountiful, fitting, first-rate, upright, noble, pleasant, skilful, reliable, lovely, beneficial, sound, considerable, commendable, loyal, adequate, choice, kind, dependable.

All can apply to who our Lord is and how he works. The Lord's nature becomes evident in what he does and how he manages it. The poet ties God's goodness with his word. No wonder that he wants to be treated according to that word and taught good judgement through it (vv. 65, 66). He confidently declares: 'You are good, and the source of good;' then asks, 'Train me in your goodness' (v. 68, *MSG*).

The psalmist appears to have learned that trouble can be beneficial when we take the opportunity it offers to learn and obey God's word (v. 67), which in turn teaches us something about our vital needs and draws us closer to God.

By contrast, he points out the proud who have lied about him – 'smeared me with lies' (v. 69) – and keeps the metaphor going by saying their hearts are 'as fat as grease' (v. 70, *NKJV*) or as dull and unfeeling as a tub of lard. They don't realise that they're only driving him closer to God.

In the end the psalmist deduces: 'My troubles turned out all for the best – they forced me to learn from your textbook' (v. 71, *MSG*). Missionary to India, E. Stanley Jones wrote: 'The way to meet unmerited suffering and injustice is not to bear them, but to use them. When I saw that possibility years ago an entirely new world opened before me. I had been trying to explain suffering, and now I saw that we are not to explain it, but to use it.'[19]

Considering the lessons the psalmist learned, it's no wonder he finds God's truth of inestimable value. 'Your instructions are more valuable to me than millions in gold and silver' (v. 72, *NLT*). Could we say the same?

Plan A

'When I left home and crossed the Jordan River, I owned nothing except a walking stick' (v. 10, NLT).

After their encounter and farewell agreement, Jacob and Laban part amiably. Jacob's relief at leaving a difficult period in Paddan Aram probably energises him as he heads for home. Yet it was under those hostile conditions that Jacob started to become sensitive to God's presence. He acknowledges that God prospered him and rewarded his faithful, reliable work. Even though Laban and his unfair treatment are behind Jacob, he can't relax.

He's heading for something he could ignore at a distance, but that he now dreads as each hill and valley bring him closer to it – meeting his estranged brother, Esau. In the midst of his worries, Jacob has an unexpected encounter with angels. Welcome back to Canaan! Perhaps seeing them reminds him of his earlier dream.

As at Bethel, the divine messengers provide him with an encouraging reminder of God's continued presence, protection and interest in his affairs. They appear on his everyday road, when most needed and in a form that heartens him. We may not see a 'camp' of God's soldiers, but God often interposes his messengers on our paths, as needed and in a form that fortifies our faith.

Reinforced, Jacob considers how to approach his brother. His first plan is to send messengers to let Esau know he is doing well and that he comes deferentially. He's seeking not aid, but reconciliation – perhaps even forgiveness. It is doubtful the messengers deliver the information, since, to Jacob's dismay, they return with news that Esau and 400 men are heading his way.

Fear rises and Jacob looks for another plan. He splits his people and animals into two groups in the hope that, if attacked, one will survive. Finally, in desperation, Jacob prays for deliverance. He admits his untenable position. His prayer amplifies his awareness of God's covenant, commands, undeserved favour, purposes and promise.

To ponder:

If we see ourselves in the equivalent of Jacob's sandals, where does prayer figure in our plans?

A Full Day

'So his gifts went before him while he settled down' (v. 21, MSG).

After Jacob acknowledges his dilemma and resorts to prayer, he sleeps (v. 13). Before the next night (v. 21) he makes changes to his earlier plan. Often prayer helps us to shift our focus and think more clearly. No longer is he paralysed by fear or desperately figuring how to mitigate defeat, but neither does he fold his arms and wait for angels to act in his stead. He wisely couples his faith in God with the resources God has given him.

Now, instead of dividing his flocks and people in two so that half of them may survive an attack, he divides them in three to be his emissaries of good will. He chooses more than 500 valuable animals as gifts for Esau, hoping for an amiable reception by the time the brothers meet. Such a sizeable gift would more than compensate Esau for what he potentially lost when Jacob tricked him out of his birthright years earlier. Restitution is an often overlooked element in the process of reconciliation.

Jacob instructs the head of each herd to deliver the same message: 'When my brother Esau comes close and asks, "Who is your master? Where are you going? Who owns these?" – answer him like this, "Your servant Jacob. They are a gift to my master Esau. He's on his way"' (vv. 17, 18, *MSG*).

Jacob is hopeful that the gifts will affect Esau's attitude. In verse 20 he says: 'I will try to appease him by sending gifts ahead of me. When I see him in person, perhaps he will be friendly to me' (*NLT*). The gifts are not a bribe. The Hebrew word for appease, *kapar*, comes from a word which initially meant 'to cover with tar' but figuratively meant to placate or cancel and, by extension, to pardon or reconcile. It carries a sense of seeking forgiveness and restoration. According to *Beacon Bible Commentary*,[20] this is the first time *kapar* is used in the Bible with this meaning.

In his extremity, Jacob turns to God and then chooses a wise, though personally costly, course. Proper priorities matter.

Jacob at Jabbok to Israel at Peniel

'The sun came up as he left Peniel' (v. 31, MSG).

We might think Jacob would sleep soundly after a full day. They're camped east of the Jordan River, about halfway between the Sea of Galilee and the Dead Sea, in a valley on the north bank of a Jordan tributary, the westward-flowing Jabbok River. Perhaps the coming encounter worries Jacob. In the night he gets everyone up, breaks camp and escorts them across a ford to the south bank. He even sends all his possessions across.

Then Jacob chooses to spend the rest of the night on the north side, alone, or so he thinks until a man wrestles with him through the rest of the night, each trying to immobilise or conquer the other. The hold the man uses on Jacob leaves him with a limp for life. Jacob is tenacious and won't let go until he receives a blessing. That blessing turns out to be a name change.

Just as God changed Jacob's grandfather and grandmother's names to Abraham and Sarah and pronounced that their child of promise would be named Isaac, Jacob 'the supplanter' receives his new name, Israel, meaning 'He struggles with God'. Perhaps he would agree that 'Prayer in its highest form and grandest success assumes the attitude of a wrestler with God.'[21]

Some biblical scholars believe the person Jacob wrestles with is the pre-incarnate Christ who appears in other instances in the Old Testament as 'the Angel of the Lord' (see Genesis 16, 22; Exodus 32; Numbers 22; Judges 6). Jacob refers to him as God (v. 30).

Appropriately, Jacob's pivotal experience takes place at the river called Jabbok, meaning pouring forth or emptying. As it flows west, it drops 3,700 feet to 1,000 feet below sea level, a radical plunge. Jacob's name change points towards just as dramatic a difference in his spirit and in his status.

On his way out Jacob named the place of his dream 'House of God'. On his return he names the place of his personal struggle with God, Peniel – 'Face of God'. Now everything is different. He may be in a valley, but the sun is rising in his life. Meeting God does that.

Warm Welcome

'And that's how it happened that Jacob arrived all in one piece in Shechem in the land of Canaan – all the way from Paddan Aram' (v. 18, MSG).

When members of our family live at a distance from us we can watch a grandchild's development via a web cam or through pictures posted online. But children we have known in various locations through the years stay frozen in time. We remember them as we last saw them and are surprised when we see them grown up.

Adults' appearances may not change as radically as children's, but our experiences and choices help to continually shape our personalities and change our outlooks. Unless we keep in touch regularly, we don't know what others have faced or how they've adjusted or grown in grace.

Jacob and Esau probably had an image of the other fixed in their mind. They probably thought the other would act exactly as they had when they parted disagreeably some twenty years earlier. Jacob moves towards meeting Esau with trepidation. In deference, he repeatedly bows when he sees his brother approaching. No wonder they both weep for joy when Esau runs to Jacob and embraces him.

Their lives have not been static. Both have done well. Jacob introduces his family to Esau. Although Esau's family did not accompany him that day, Genesis 36 tells us about them. Esau protests about the lavish gifts Jacob sent ahead to him. But Jacob insists that if Esau heartily welcomes him, he should prove it by accepting these gifts. He goes further: 'When I saw your face, it was as the face of God smiling on me' (v. 10, *MSG*). The genial meeting was that much of a relief. He may also think of his recent meeting with God at the place he'd named 'Face of God' (32:30).

Jacob again senses that God is continuing to make a way for him. The altar he builds and calls 'Mighty is the God of Israel' is one outward expression. When we witness God's providential care through the years, how do we witness to it?

Course Correction via Obedience

'Jacob called the place where God had talked with him Bethel' (v. 15).

The impulsive actions of Simeon and Levi in chapter 34 bring dishonour to God and grief to their father. Throughout the incident Jacob shows little leadership or parental oversight. And Jacob, who earlier was so ready to recompense his brother, shows little concern for the victims of his sons' treachery. He's more concerned with his reputation.

Whether his family is now in danger or just disgraced, in Jacob's time of need and sensitivity God graciously calls him to move his family away from Shechem. Sometimes distance can be palliative.

God gives Jacob a second chance to go where he should have gone sooner, to Bethel, only thirty miles away. Since his return, Jacob has not yet fulfilled the vow he'd made decades earlier when God met him in his distress as he set out for Paddan Aram (28:20–22). God has provided, but Jacob has neglected to fulfil his promises. When God supplies our needs, do we remember the promises we made in less comfortable times? Jacob is to go to Bethel with his family and build an altar. Now Jacob acts decisively as a leader.

Jacob knows what to do. He states his plan, course of action and his rationale. He insists that his household come clean. They must rid themselves of idols of all sorts and any practices associated with them. He implies that until now he's tolerated the family's mixed religious loyalties, but no longer. They must each sense the gravity of preparing to worship an all-powerful God. They give Jacob not only their idols, but even their personal good-luck charms of jewellery (v. 4). He buries all these items near Shechem. Then they set out.

After his sons' treachery, Jacob may wonder if neighbouring tribes will unite and take revenge. But as they move ahead in obedience, they're miraculously shielded by God's providential care. When they come to Bethel and Jacob obediently erects the altar, God reaffirms Jacob's name, ratifies the covenant and makes fresh promises of nations, kings and land for Jacob's descendants.

Losses and a Gain

'The God of Abraham and Isaac and Jacob, the God of our ancestors, has glorified his Son Jesus' (Acts 3:13, MSG).

Bethel, the place of covenant and promise for Jacob, is also a burial place (v. 8). Deborah had served Jacob's mother since before Rebekah married Isaac (24:59). Deborah may have been the midwife for Jacob and Esau. She is mourned as family. Apparently Rebekah had already died as well. But there are other losses Jacob could ponder, such as his daughter Dinah's rape and the lives of the men of Shechem, whom his sons murdered.

As the company leaves Bethel and heads south for Hebron, where aged Isaac lives, Jacob may well wonder when he will lose his father as well. Sometimes around the time when an elderly family member dies, a child is born to the offspring. How many sons will he introduce to his father? Amazingly, Jacob's wife, Rachel, is pregnant again, so perhaps there will be twelve.

Then, while they're travelling Rachel goes into labour. In the midst of her pain, her midwife reminds Rachel that when Joseph was born she prayed that God would give her another son (30:24) and now she is delivering him. Rachel dies naming him Ben-Oni, 'Son of my sorrow' (35:18).

Jacob breaks precedent and renames him Benjamin, literally 'Son of the right hand'. The position at someone's right hand was a place of honour. Another explanation of the name is that people usually faced east to give directions, so south was to the right. This child was the only one in Jacob's family born south of Haran and on a southerly trek. His name could mean southerner. He is youngest, but not least; King Saul and the apostle Paul came from the tribe of Benjamin. Jacob buries Rachel and sets up a monument to her.

Finally Jacob reaches his father and a peaceful homecoming. He's there when his father dies at age 180. History repeats itself as Jacob and Esau join in burying Isaac as the once estranged brothers Isaac and Ishmael had their father, Abraham. Jacob is the patriarch now. God would be known as the God of Abraham, Isaac and Jacob.

J – Jod

*'Now comfort me so I can live, really live; your revelation is
the tune I dance to' (vv. 77, MSG).*

On this Lord's Day, with the psalmist we acknowledge the One who
created us – body, mind and soul – and confidently ask him, the source
of our capacities, to help us use the intelligence he's given us to understand
his commands and the wisdom to live accordingly (v. 73).

When we show that we pin our hopes on his word to us, others are
encouraged (v. 74). What are some of the ways this happens? In a meeting
or a small group we occasionally hear someone testify to their experience
of believing God's word, obeying what the Spirit says to their hearts and
finding satisfaction when the Lord works through them. More often our
inspiration comes from reading about someone's faith in action in a
Christian book, magazine, newsletter or blog.

Possibly what moves us most to also be 'doers of the word' is hearing
examples of faith in God's Word in natural everyday conversations with
other believers. Since that's a blessing to us, perhaps we should ask the
Lord to keep us alert to similar opportunities to mention the help we're
finding in his Word.

Verses 75, 76 and 77 seem to belong together. In verse 75 there's the
declaration that God's righteousness is seen in his standards; then the
concession that when he humbles us (as the word for 'afflicts' can read),
it's an expression of his faithfulness.

When the psalmist asks God to demonstrate divine loving kindness by
comforting him and divine compassionate mercy by surrounding him, we
think of the Lord's promise in Isaiah 66:13: 'As a mother comforts her
child, so I'll comfort you' (*MSG*). The psalmist says the purpose for such
parental care is to enable us to live an abundant life as we delight in God's
word and way.

I write these comments on a rainy 9/11 Day of Remembrance and
Service in the USA, and as they are being read it is Remembrance Sunday
in the United Kingdom. The God of all comfort is with us.

Jacob's Naïve Dreamer

*'So Jacob settled again in the land of Canaan, where his father
had lived as a foreigner' (v. 1, NLT).*

When Isaac dies, Jacob's family settles in the Hebron Valley where his father and grandparents had lived and were buried. It is the land to which Abraham was called and lies in what the Israelites would one day claim as their Promised Land. From chapter 37 the focus of Genesis shifts from Jacob to Joseph, but we will continue to follow Jacob's part and perspective in the unfolding story.

Jacob's sons tend his growing flocks and at times their search for pasture takes them a distance from home. As a teenager, Joseph sometimes works with his older brothers Dan, Naphtali, Gad and Asher – sons of the maids of Rachel his mother and Leah, Jacob's other wife.

Joseph may be his father's favourite by no fault of his own. Jacob loved Rachel most and although Joseph was the eleventh son born to the household, he was her first-born. Perhaps Jacob can glimpse a bit of Rachel in Joseph. Or perhaps Jacob sees he has wisdom beyond his years (one meaning for the phrase, 'son of old age' – v. 3). Jacob's gift of special clothing to Joseph doesn't help. It's a further mark of favouritism and distinction.

But part of his brothers' resentment of Joseph is of his own making. He tattles on them. He is also naïve or indiscreet in describing his dreams in which he always plays the starring role.

Although Jacob rebukes Joseph, perhaps he understands. At critical times in his life God spoke to Jacob and guided him through dreams: when he left home and while he served Laban. Joseph's jealous brothers hate him and can't speak civilly to him, but Jacob ponders the whole issue; keeps the matter in mind (v. 11). Maturity and life experience bring wisdom, especially when partnered with a growing awareness of God and his purposes.

What will the family think many years later, when within God's plan and to their benefit, the seemingly arrogant dreams of youth turn out to have been prophetic?

Broken Dreams

'The LORD is close to the broken-hearted and saves those who are crushed in spirit' (Psalm 34:18).

The drama develops. Some of Jacob's sons take his flocks to forage near Shechem. Jacob recalls the earlier trouble his sons wreaked in Shechem and wants to be sure they're safe. He chooses Joseph to go the sixty miles north to check. In no time Joseph is ready and wears the special cloak that bothers his brothers.

A few days later when Joseph arrives in the area and doesn't find his brothers, on the word of a friendly stranger who heard they were moving on to Dothan, Joseph travels on. They see him coming and conspire to kill the dreamer. The eldest, Reuben, protests and suggests putting Joseph in a pit to die. He plans to rescue him secretly later. Is he worried about his father's reaction or does he fear being held responsible?

They attack the dreamer, rip off his coat and put him in the pit. While Reuben is temporarily out of sight, the brothers indifferently eat a meal until another of Leah's sons, Judah, comes up with a different plan. They won't hurt him; just sell him to the passing spice caravan headed for Egypt. The memory of the scent of myrrh and balm from Gilead, embalming spices, would haunt the brothers and outlast the silver they received in exchange for Joseph. Simple cues can continue to prick conscience long after a deed.

Reuben finds Joseph gone and despairs. In further treachery they kill a goat – one from Jacob's flocks – for blood to smear on the coat, then take it home as if they have found it. According to plan, their father concludes that an animal killed his son. Not even Reuben counters the false assumption or dares to speak the truth.

Until we come to sincere repentance, one sin often leads to another and unnecessarily spreads hurt and pain. Jacob is heartbroken and mourns deeply for a long time. Without the truth, nothing anyone says or does helps; he weeps inconsolably and wears the coarse burlap clothes of a mourner. He's lost his Rachel, and now Joseph.

To ponder:

Only God can heal a broken heart. Only truth sets us free.

Coatless to Royal Robe

'So Pharaoh asked his officials, "Can we find anyone else like this man so obviously filled with the spirit of God?"' (v. 38, NLT).

Jacob bemoans his loss and regrets ever sending Joseph to check on the flocks and family. Meanwhile seventeen-year-old Joseph is taken south to Egypt where he is sold as a slave to an officer of Pharaoh's guard. Joseph prospers in his new setting; his success is due to the Lord's blessing (39:2–6).

Joseph's reaction to trouble is very different from his brothers'. Besides the plots they hatch to do away with Joseph and deceive their father, their jealousy, hatred and lust lead to murder (chapter 34), incest (35:22) and irresponsible immorality (chapter 38).

On the other hand, even though thrust into difficult situations not of his making – out of touch with his home culture, language and family, in servitude among strangers, falsely accused, forgotten – Joseph exhibits moral strength, courage, kindness, honesty and confidence in God. His life is an example to us in our own challenging circumstances. Further, commentators find dozens of similarities between the lives of Joseph and Jesus. In some ways Joseph prefigures Christ, our perfect example.

After thirteen years as a slave or in prison, at age thirty Joseph receives an elevated position of service to the king (41:40, 46). It all stems from his reliance on God's presence in his life, consistent living and faithfulness in relaying what God reveals to him. The king gives Joseph symbols of power, dresses him in royal clothes and arranges for his marriage (vv. 42, 45).

In his new role Joseph supervises the stewardship of agriculture during the years of prosperity in preparation for the coming years of famine foretold by God through Pharaoh's dreams. When the food crisis comes, Egypt is ready.

During the time of abundance Joseph and his wife Asenath have two sons whom he names Manasseh ('Forgetfulness') and Ephraim ('Fruitfulness'), for Joseph wisely concludes that God caused him to forget his earlier hardships and made him prosper in the land of his affliction.

What Next?

'All the ways of the LORD are loving and faithful for those who keep the demands of his covenant' (Psalm 25:10).

We don't hear about Jacob for more than twenty years. But when the desperate situation of famine in the whole region turns his attention to where there is grain available, Egypt, he dispatches ten of his sons there to buy food. He won't let Benjamin go. Perhaps he needs Benjamin to oversee the flocks during his brothers' absence of at least several weeks.

The party runs into difficulties in Egypt when the man in charge seems suspicious of their motives. Joseph recognises them, but it isn't mutual. Joseph wears different clothes, is clean-shaven, speaks a different language and seems to be Egyptian.

He acts like the stranger they think he is in order to test them and discern their motives. He is heartened when they give truthful answers and is deeply moved at Reuben's confession that the way they unjustly treated Joseph years before is now boomeranging. Nothing is as hard to suppress as a guilty conscience. He keeps them in prison for three days, then releases them conditionally; the youngest brother must come with them next time.

Simeon is kept behind to ensure they return and the rest are sent back to Jacob with grain and, secretly, the money they paid for it. When the money is discovered, the brothers take it as an act of God (v. 28).

They return home with the needed grain. But when the nine give their father an honest account of what transpired in Egypt, Jacob feels worse. It's their fault he's lost Joseph and now Simeon. No wonder he refuses to consider the demand to take Benjamin and says everything is going against him (v. 36). Rashly, Reuben offers his own sons' lives in exchange for Benjamin's safety. But Jacob is adamant. Benjamin is not leaving. Losing him would kill Jacob (v. 38). Nothing can persuade him – yet. They watch the grain deplete. Perhaps they eat less to delay the inevitable trip. But God is also present in days of uncertainty.

The Non-Routine Trip

'The men took the gifts, double the money and Benjamin.
They lost no time in getting to Egypt and meeting Joseph' (v. 15, MSG).

When Jacob can no longer put off the inevitable he is forced to send his sons back to Egypt for grain. Judah reminds him that the ruler there insists on seeing their youngest brother this time. Jacob protests that they should never have mentioned Benjamin, but Judah offers to be guarantor of Benjamin's safe return. Since the welfare of the whole family is at stake, Jacob reluctantly agrees.

The patriarch insists that they return the silver they'd found in their sacks as well as take more to pay for whatever grain they might be able to buy. He also sends the ruler gifts. Although gifts turned out not to have been necessary when he first met his brother Esau again, they hadn't hurt either. He's still relying on his best efforts even when things are really out of his control.

Jacob adds his fervent desire, that God would grant them mercy in Egypt (43:14), yet he seems resigned to loss. The drama intensifies when the eleven brothers arrive in Egypt. Chapters 43 and 44 reveal that Joseph treats them far better than they deserve. Through further tests, he wisely determines that they are telling the truth about their family, that they are dealing honestly with him and that they are trustworthy.

When Judah details their situation up to the moment and offers to remain in Egypt as a slave rather than break his father's heart again, Joseph is convinced. Judah, who hatched the plan to sell Joseph, is willing to be a slave himself to save Benjamin. Judah, who lied to Jacob about Joseph's fate, now courageously shows his loyalty to Jacob at personal cost.

The suspense Joseph allowed reaches its limit as he dismisses everyone except his brothers and wails and weeps loudly. At last he reveals his true identity: 'I am Joseph!' It's a nightmare the brothers couldn't have imagined. Now they are truly terrified and speechless (45:3). They are stripped of all hope unless God honours their father's desire and shows them mercy in Egypt.

Reconciled

*'But God sent me ahead of you to preserve for you a remnant on
earth and to save your lives by a great deliverance' (v. 7).*

After he reveals who he is, Joseph asks his brothers about his father, as
he had when they arrived with their gifts (43:28). Perhaps they back
away in fear when he calls them to come closer, for Egyptians do not
associate closely with Hebrews. However, Joseph then urges them not to be
hard on themselves for what they'd done to him. He does not berate them,
blame them or try to get even with them.

Joseph neither excuses what they did nor says it was inevitable. Instead
he expresses forgiveness and gives God glory for overruling their actions
and making it possible for him now to provide for them and rescue the
whole family from starvation. Reconciliation sets restoration in motion.

He wants them to quickly bring their father to Egypt. Joseph wants to
see to Jacob's care himself. His plan is for the whole clan and all their
animals to move to a region of Egypt where during the remaining years of
famine he can use the privileged position God has given him for their
benefit. When Pharaoh hears of the reunion, he's delighted and insists that
the brothers take gifts to the family and bring everyone back to Egypt.
They don't need to bring all their belongings; Egypt's finest will be at their
disposal (v. 20).

These aren't empty words. Pharaoh supplies the wagons to make trans-
porting elderly Jacob and those who could have been overlooked – the
women and children – easier (v. 19). It's wonderful when someone
thoughtfully anticipates a need and unconditionally offers a practical,
caring way to meet it. Such service is Jesus' way.

———

To pray:

**Jesus, help me to let your thoughtful, watchful, wise, unselfish, helpful, kind love
touch others through me.**

K – *Kaph*

'In your great love revive me so I can alertly obey your every word'
(v. 88, MSG).

This portion of Psalm 119 paints a mostly grey picture. The psalmist has looked and waited so long for God's promised deliverance that his eyes can't focus and he feels faint. That sounds like the condition of someone who's starving. In his exhaustion he describes himself as a shrivelled wineskin bottle – parched and shrunken, useless.

The plaintiff asks how long he has to wait for comfort to come and the cause of his unwarranted maltreatment to end. He claims that his tormentors, who have not only tried to sidetrack him with lies, have nearly succeeded in killing him.

Yet this tattered, battered, weary supplicant holds on. His situation, his surroundings and he himself are hopeless. Yet he hopes in something stable outside himself – God's dependable word. He remembers it, affirms it as trustworthy and does not turn away from it. As grim as the situation is, he clings to the right things. He asks for help in the right places. He asks God to act according to his love. If the Lord will keep him alive, the writer promises to obey what he says.

For most of us things aren't usually this bleak, although they may seem so at times. Telling us to cheer up doesn't help. Sometimes a good lament is just what's needed. If we do it as the psalmists did, at some point we'll turn from pouring out our colourless bewildering dilemmas to recognising God's full-colour, loving interest and willingness to help us. He works in myriad ways in answer to our prayers, and gives us fresh outlooks.

Today is Thanksgiving Sunday in the USA. Whether we live in regions where harvest is safely stored, spring is in full bloom, or it's perpetually summer or winter, we can together turn with hymnwriter Isaac Watts to God, 'our help in ages past, our hope for years to come', asking him to be evident in our todays, as well as our dwelling place forever.

Life-Changing News

*'Do not be afraid to go down to Egypt, for I will make you into
a great nation there' (v. 3).*

After twelve brothers who were separated for more than twenty years are reconciled, eleven return home with the grain, special gifts and amazing news. Perhaps they hope their father will understand how they feel. Years earlier he too was reunited with his estranged brother, Esau, after a twenty-year separation.

Jacob is most concerned for the safe return of his sons – especially Simeon who had been held in prison, and his youngest, Benjamin. What more can he ask than that?

Then they tell him that Joseph is alive and is a ruler in Egypt. Jacob can't believe it; his heart stands still (v. 27). But when they relate what Joseph said and show him the carts he has sent to transport the family, Jacob begins to believe them and revives. For Jacob it's as if Joseph has been resurrected. What Jacob thought hopeless and out of his control was really under God's care.

A long-burdened father is jubilant. If it's true Joseph lives, Jacob will go to him at once. Change, especially when it involves moving to an unknown place, can be daunting for anyone, and more so for someone who is 130. But Jacob is highly motivated. He doesn't want to die without seeing Joseph again.

Before going to Egypt, Jacob makes an important stop. Perhaps he has second thoughts about leaving Canaan – the Promised Land. Or perhaps he remembers what happened when his grandfather took a detour in Egypt. And God had specifically told his father, Isaac, not to go to Egypt. With all this in mind he stops in Beersheba to worship God and no doubt seek God's guidance and blessing.

That night Jacob has his answer. God speaks to Jacob in a way familiar to him – through a vision. God is clear. Jacob should go to Egypt. Further, God promises to make his family a great nation; to be with him and bring him back; and assures him Joseph will be with him when he dies. Doubt is gone. He moves out trusting God.

Jacob's Ultimate Move

'Counting in the two sons born to Joseph in Egypt, the members of Jacob's family who ended up in Egypt numbered seventy' (v. 27, MSG).

Jacob heads for Egypt as excited as a child on an outing. It's never too late to embrace hope. His family will have a safe place to live with plenty of food for them and their animals during the famine and return to the Promised Land in the future. He will see Joseph before he dies. Most importantly, God will be with him.

Jacob moves his entire household – goods, flocks and all his offspring. Those unable to walk or ride donkeys go by wagon. The caravan's progress moves at the pace of the slowest oxen.

It is interesting that the list of Jacob's children is categorised according to their mothers, the grandchildren according to their fathers. Today, Orthodox and Conservative Judaism hold that one is Jewish only if one's mother is Jewish, while some movements of Judaism maintain either a patrilineal or a bilineal view. In the Gospels, the genealogies of Christ include fathers and some mothers.

The record of Jacob's offspring includes sixty-six names, and if we add Jacob, Joseph and Joseph's two sons, the total is seventy. Such a small number can hardly seem significant compared with the tribes and nations of the day. We see through Scripture that God can use all who obey him, but often chooses to work through the few.

It takes generations to prepare Israel to become a people of God, to increase the seventy to upwards of two million, to bring the leader of a mass migration to the forefront. This stage of the story depends on Jacob's trust in God and willingness to move forward at his word.

Near Egypt, Jacob chooses Judah to meet Joseph and work out the details of the party's arrival. It is the fifth time Judah has travelled this route with his brothers. But he no longer travels it as the selfish man he once was. In spite of past failures, he has shown that he is sacrificial and dependable. Jacob reflects the grace of the God of second chances in giving Judah the trusted role of emissary.

Beyond Our Dreams

'His power at work in us can do far more than we dare ask or imagine'
(Ephesians 3:20, CEV).

Jacob's family is directed to Goshen, a large fertile acreage in the Nile Delta region. We imagine Jacob's anticipation mounting as his lengthy wagon trip ends. News of the family's arrival sends Joseph's long-deferred hope into action and he uses the speediest method available to reach them. Finally their longings merge in a joyful, tearful reunion.

A dozen years ago my husband and I were moved at the wedding of one of our sons as we watched him wait as his bride walked towards him. Rather than standing stoical or beaming, he was weeping with joy to receive her at last. This isn't the first time we've seen Joseph weeping for joy.

When we long for, plan for and work towards something and then, even though it seems too good to be true, it actually happens, the emotional release can be tremendous and uncontrollable. Joseph embraces his father for a long time. Jacob says he's ready to die, as though his life's mission is complete now that the son he'd lost is found.

Jacob's words remind us of another elderly Jew's song aeons later. When Simeon saw the infant Jesus at the temple, he was thankful that God had kept his promise and allowed him to see his salvation in his lifetime. Simeon was satisfied and ready for the Lord to release him. Jacob's dreams have come true, and he will live for another seventeen years enjoying his now complete family in a land of sunshine and plenty – quite the retirement plan.

Joseph provides visas to enter Egypt, but permission for more permanent residency must come from Pharaoh. Joseph advises his brothers that Pharaoh needs to be assured of their intentions and occupations. The five brothers Joseph chooses meet Pharaoh and quickly gain not only his permission to settle in Goshen, but an offer of employment. As we move at God's direction, he thoroughly prepares the way.

The Pilgrim

'Israel worshipped as he leaned on the top of his staff' (v. 31).

The delegation of Joseph's brothers receives Pharaoh's approval and gains their desired settlement location. Joseph wants to introduce his father to the benevolent sovereign who has treated him well. Jacob has been the overseer of his expanding family and their livelihood since he left his unsympathetic father-in-law's contractual service in distant Paddan Aram decades earlier. Now in a foreign land with customs that are new to him, he's about to meet its powerful ruler. Is he intimidated?

One autumn the New York Yankees were in the baseball World Series. Their stated game plan was to play excellent ball. Their implied plan was to intimidate the visiting team with the dazzle of New York City, celebrity spectators and the team's legendary history. In the opening game with the Philadelphia Phillies none of the strategy worked. The Phillies' pitcher wasn't unnerved by New York. He said he'd played baseball all his life and just did what he knew how to do. His team won.

Jacob also meets the Pharaoh with that kind of assurance. The Pharaoh is revered in his land as a son of the sun god. But Jacob has personally encountered the one true God and is in covenant with him. The Pharaoh holds power over his country, but Jacob holds promises of provision and protection from God.

When Joseph presents his father, Jacob blesses Pharaoh. Perhaps this means Jacob gives the basic expected polite greeting of the culture before conversing. Or perhaps Jacob, acting as patriarch, is also confidently asking God's blessing on the benevolent king. In response to the ruler's question, the 130-year-old Jacob states his age and includes the apt description of his life as a pilgrimage.

Having a pilgrim's outlook affects how we regard our possessions, our relationships, even life and death. Jacob lives another seventeen years. When Jacob senses his life is nearly over, he exacts a vow from Joseph – that he'll be buried with his ancestors. As soon as Joseph commits to Jacob's request, Jacob quite naturally worships God.

Double Blessings

'Then Israel said to Joseph, "I am about to die, but God will be with you and take you back to the land of your fathers" ' (v. 21).

When Jacob's health dramatically declines, Joseph and his sons visit him. He struggles to sit up to receive them, so he can say some important things. He recalls the first time God appeared to him and made a personal covenant with him. He testifies to this as a prelude to his formal adoption of Joseph's two sons whom Jacob means to include in the covenant blessing. Jacob puts the boys on a par with Reuben and Simeon, Jacob's firstborn. By adopting his grandsons as his own, Jacob can pass a double blessing to Joseph.

Nearly blind Jacob hugs Manasseh and Ephraim and says to Joseph, 'I never expected to see your face again, and now God has allowed me to see your children too' (v. 11) – a double blessing.

Then Joseph stands the boys in place for his father's blessing – eldest to the right, youngest to the left. Jacob purposely puts his right hand on Ephraim's head and crosses his left over to Manasseh as he pronounces his blessing. Joseph tries to correct his father, but Jacob has acted knowingly. 'Fruitfulness' (Ephraim) precedes 'Forgetfulness' (Manasseh). For the third time in the patriarchal line the younger son overtakes the place of the older.

The blessing Jacob pronounces is also his testimony. The Lord who initiated the covenant with Abraham, the God of Jacob's fathers, has been both Jacob's trusted shepherd and angel of deliverance throughout his life. He wants no less for Ephraim and Manasseh.

As an extra boon, Jacob pledges Joseph a specific ridge of land in the Promised Land (v. 22). New Testament writers still knew where it was – in Samaria near Sychar, where Jesus met the woman at the well (John 4:5).

Jacob knows his life is almost over. He focuses on what God will do in his children's lives. He says God will be with them and will take them back to the land of promise (v. 21). The twofold promise would steady them in trying days ahead. The promise of God's presence and provision still stabilises us in our Egypt experiences.

Bad Intentions Overruled

'You intended to harm me, but God intended it for good to accomplish what is now being done, the saving of many lives' (50:20).

Although Genesis 49 is sometimes referred to as Jacob blessing his sons (v. 28), Jacob only really uses the word 'bless' when he refers to Joseph (vv. 25, 26) whom he elevates above all the others. The chapter is more a record of the state of the family than a farewell. Jacob gathers all his sons for a rich blend of memorable metaphors, son by son. Artists such as Marc Chagall and Phillip Ratner have colourfully depicted each image in family-crest-like form.

Some of Jacob's speech reveals what his sons already know; some of it predicts what will unfold through their descendants, the twelve tribes; some of it offers vision and promise. Whether as word pictures or works of art, the twelve depictions are rich in meaning and prophecy.

Jacob's final address is an illustration of his faith that God will continue to work through his offspring. When Jacob finishes, he again specifies his burial place, trusting that in life and in death his family will remember Canaan. Then, satisfied, he composes himself as if for a snooze and dies at age 137 surrounded by his family.

Joseph weeps unashamedly, and then arranges for Egyptian embalming and mourning for Jacob. Afterwards he asks permission to take Jacob's body back to Canaan. The Pharaoh agrees and sends all the dignitaries of Egypt to the funeral. Chariots and horses accompany. Jacob is honoured in death.

With their father dead, Joseph's older brothers fear what Joseph will do to them. They plead for forgiveness. Joseph acknowledges their wrong but quickly adds that God has overruled the evil they planned and brought good out of it that benefits many – even them. Like the God he follows, Joseph is gracious and forgiving. He will take care of them.

Before Joseph dies at age 110 he asks that, when God takes Jacob's progeny out of Egypt, they take his bones with them. His request is an expression of his faith in God's plan and goodness. Years later he is buried in Canaan.

L – *Lamed*

'I see a limit to all things, but thy law has a boundless range' (v. 96, JMT).

The classics can mean a branch of the humanities which studies aspects of ancient, foundational cultures. Classical music can denote music composed or rooted in traditional forms over many centuries. In some places, classic cars are historic vehicles, so it's a matter of age, but elsewhere the quality and quantity of the cars also contribute to their classic status. A classic book might be one that most people think should be read by all for either its enduring value or modern significance. Clothes that don't go out of style are dubbed classic.

But the ultimate 'classic' is God's Word. In today's segment of the psalm, the writer says that God's Word is as permanent as the heavens, his truth as dependable as the sunrise. The earth's continued existence and operation relies on the laws God created.

The psalmist testifies that adhering to what God says has been the difference between life and death for him. Since he's proved it reliable when he's been in trouble, he intends to keep holding on to this lifeline.

More than enduring over generations and being tested and proven personally, he sees God's Word as inexhaustible. On this first Sunday of Advent, we concur that everything human has limits, but rejoice that God's Word and the Word Made Flesh are limitless.

> That word above all earthly powers,
> No thanks to them abideth;
> The Spirit and the gifts are ours
> Through him who with us sideth.
> Let goods and kindred go,
> This mortal life also;
> The body they may kill;
> God's truth abideth still,
> His Kingdom is for ever.
> *Martin Luther* (*SASB* 1)

Come, Emmanuel!

Introduction

Our house is near a freight-train crossing. Whether a train goes north or south along the single track, the law requires the engineer to sound the horn four times before entering the crossing. Whether he blows a gentle or forceful warning, we know when a train is approaching. Just as surely, the four weeks of Advent herald Christmas.

The Advent (literally 'arrival') season begins on the Sunday closest to St Andrew's Day, 30 November. Since children's excitement about Christmas builds daily, some parents provide an Advent calendar to help keep the month at a measured pace for them. One father finds that lighting the Advent wreath and singing a verse of 'O come, O come, Emmanuel' at supper each evening is meaningful and has a calming effect on his family.

For seventeen centuries or more, believers have approached Christmas through Advent, the time of preparation. The focus has been on three comings: the coming of Christ to earth – we live on a visited planet; the coming of Christ to the human heart – we can individually know his presence; and Christ's anticipated second coming – we live hopefully.

During the current Advent, primarily using Luke 1 and 2, we will consider some of the key players involved in Christ's first advent. Their reactions to the good news vary. Some of their questions and responses may reflect ours.

We sing in anticipation and affirmation:

> O come, O come, Emmanuel,
> And ransom captive Israel,
> That mourns in lonely exile here
> Until the Son of God appear.
>
> Rejoice! Rejoice!
> Emmanuel shall come to thee, O Israel.
>
> (From twelfth-century Latin antiphons,
> trs. John M. Neale)

Waiting

*'So you, too, must keep watch! For you do not know the day
or hour of my return' (v.13, NLT).*

Some of us are better 'waiters' than others. That partly depends on how we wait, what we're waiting for and how long we wait. Fear makes waiting especially difficult. We all wait at times.

All the key players in the drama in the opening of Luke's Gospel are waiting – Elizabeth and Zechariah, Anna, Simeon, Mary and Joseph. Do they wait resignedly or expectantly, passively or actively? They seem to wait patiently. They were all part of a people who had been waiting for centuries for the Messiah. The Old Testament is full of references to waiting.

Perhaps Luke's characters are patient waiters because they know that the one who promised a Messiah is reliable. They aren't the 'climb every mountain, 'til you find your dream' sort, but the more contemplative, 'be still and know' type.

Their time and culture may have helped to form their outlook. They weren't free to set a course for self-actualisation or achievement. But they could choose their outlook – chafing or trusting. They're willing to stay put until they see the fulfilment of the promise.

They aren't merely wishful thinkers. Their attitude is costly and courageous. Against prevalent views to the contrary, they know that God will come through, so they hope on.

The Christian community also waits. Today we wait in expectation. We encourage each other to stay alert to the Word and awake and ready in our day-to-day lives. Jesus told us to keep watch and be faithful in small things. No one else may notice, but he will and, after all, he's the one we're waiting for – and the wait will be worth it.

Specially Placed

'And they both were righteous in the sight of God, walking blamelessly in all the commandments and requirements of the Lord' (v.6, AB).

Luke writes to Theophilus (literally, lover of God) for the purpose of helping him to be sure of the facts of the life of Christ. Luke was not an eyewitness to Jesus' ministry, but he carefully researched the many digests (like blogs of the day) circulating at the time and then set the verifiable facts down in his Gospel. Luke's care with the details gives us, also lovers of God, the majority of our insights into events surrounding the birth of Jesus.

That includes the birth of John the Baptist who was born six months before Jesus. Both of John's parents were descendants of priests, and Zechariah was himself a priest. They obeyed God's commandments and paid attention to religious ordinances. Scripture calls them 'blameless'. Of course, they were not without sin, but they knew what to do when they failed the Lord's standard. *The Message* says they enjoyed a clear conscience before God.

Since Zechariah and Elizabeth were elderly, they probably were examples of people who knew how to treat others and to walk with God. They remind us of older faithful believers we know. They may have memorised favourite Scripture verses, songs and prayers and incorporated them into their daily routines.

The Abijah division of priests, the one to which Zechariah belonged, was on duty at the temple for two weeks each year. This time, probably for the only time in his life, Zechariah *happened* to be chosen to burn the temple incense. Not only did the incense he burned symbolise the prayers of the people, but at the same time, the mass standing outside were praying. Among other things, they were likely praying for him. He was specially placed.

If we pause to pray for those who serve the Lord on our behalf, even as they minister, they'll be encouraged, supported and better equipped to continue. We'll be blessed as well.

Unexpected News

'Then the angel said, "I am Gabriel! I stand in the very presence of God. It was he who sent me to bring you this good news!" ' (v.19, NLT).

The old man, accustomed to life in Judah's relatively quiet hill country, was in the bustling city of Jerusalem. Was it exciting or wearying, or both? Zechariah probably missed Elizabeth. While Zechariah is ministering in his unique opportunity, the Lord's messenger breaks into his world. We aren't surprised that Zechariah is startled. No prophetic or angelic message for 400 years, why now? He's a priest in his sunset years, why to him? He's possibly new to heady temple incense duty, why in this atmosphere? It's the time of public prayer, why at this hour?

He's scared to death, so the angel reassuringly urges him not to be afraid. His prayer is heard. Which prayer, he may wonder, for Israel's deliverance or for his very private desire for a child? If this angel knows what Zechariah prays for, he must be God-sent.

Gabriel launches into detail. Elizabeth will have a son. Call him John. He'll be a delight to you. His birth will bring joy to many. He'll be great in God's eyes. Rather than intoxicating drink, he'll be filled with God's Spirit. He'll bring many back to the Lord. He'll precede the Lord as his forerunner to prepare people for him.

The encounter carries many implications. The message comes to a priest. Jesus will come as our everlasting priest (Hebrews 7:25). It occurs during worship in the temple, a symbol of God's presence. It's in Jerusalem, the city of David, the city of God, the city of Christ's crucifixion and resurrection.

If what the angel says is true, Zechariah's prayers both for his people and for his family will be answered. We'd expect that the old man might ask to hear this again or be speechless, but instead he registers logical disbelief. Now as a verifying sign and a daily reminder of his doubt, he really is speechless. When he reappears before the crowd, and they can tell he's seen something extraordinary, he is mute so can only gesture to convey the experience.

To ponder:

Does restriction offer the urgency of sharing God's message?

Open-Handed Response

'I belong to the Lord, body and soul . . . let it happen as you say' (v. 38, JBP).

About six months after he delivered God's message to Zechariah, Gabriel appears again. The two missions are related. Although they have some things in common, there are definite differences too.

Both times the angel comes with a specific message to a specific individual. Both appearances astound and initially frighten, as the unexpected often does. Both times he reassures the recipient by name before proceeding with the startling news. Both announcements involve the promise of a child's birth including what to name that child. Both recipients recognise the impossibility for natural reasons.

But in the first case the angel appears in a bustling metropolis; in the second in a quiet town. In the first he brings his news to someone carrying out his religious duties in a place of worship; in the second to someone by herself, possibly at home. One recipient is an old man; the other a young woman.

Zechariah's response to the message is, 'How can I be sure of this? I am an old man and my wife is well on in years' (v. 18). His question reveals an attitude of doubt and seems to seek a sign. However, Mary's response, 'How will this be . . . since I am a virgin?' (v. 34) isn't one of disbelief but of wanting to know more. So Zechariah gets his sign – he's mute for months. But Mary gets an answer – she'll become pregnant when God's Spirit and power mysteriously and miraculously hover over her.

The two announcements converge when Gabriel further reassures Mary that God can do anything and tells her of Zechariah and Elizabeth's incredible news.

When Mary responds to Gabriel and says that she's God's servant and is willing (v. 38), we sense that she bows her head along with her heart. Someone has said that this was not hopeless resignation or a determined attitude to get through the ordeal with clenched fists, but an open-handed relinquishment coupled with an attitude of looking forward to what God would do. Such an attitude is one we can emulate.

Sanctuary and Training for Mission

'You are blessed because you believed that the Lord would do what he said'
(v. 45, NLT).

In our comments two days ago we left dumbstruck Zechariah finishing his duties in Jerusalem. Before he left home, he may have planned to bring back a detailed account of his opportunities at the temple and experiences in the city. Little did he know he would see an angel and be given a life-changing message. Once Elizabeth got over his loss of speech, he would need to find a way to relate everything to her. Gestures alone wouldn't do.

Elizabeth did conceive and chose to go into seclusion. In verse 24 *The Message* says: 'She went off by herself for five months, relishing her pregnancy.' All the changes to body and emotions were new to her. They were welcome, but she needed time to adjust to them. Today she would turn off her mobile phone and stay away from social networking venues. Some things are too personal and sacred for the Web.

Six months later, when as part of the angel's breathtaking message Mary finds out about her cousin's news, she wastes no time in setting out on the seventy-mile trek to visit Elizabeth, who was probably the only one who could begin to fathom Mary's situation. Mary may have meant to surprise her pregnant cousin. As she enters the house, and before either woman can share her news, at Mary's initial greeting Elizabeth's unborn child jumps and Elizabeth is filled with the Spirit. Some commentators suggest this was in fulfilment of the promise to Zechariah in verse 15 that the couple's child would be sensible of the Holy Spirit even in the womb. John welcomed Christ from the start.

Elizabeth blurted out a spontaneous holy affirmation of Mary and her child, and only God knew how much it meant to Mary to hear her cousin's unsolicited verification of her private extraordinary blessing. Mary stayed three months in the sanctuary of this affirming home, leaving around the time John was born and returning to her own home to face God's mission solely for her.

Season of Dilemma

'When Joseph woke up, he did what the angel of the Lord had commanded him and took Mary home as his wife' (v. 24).

Mary isn't the only one affected by Gabriel's announcement. Her fiancé, Joseph, must have struggled with the news and wrestled with how to handle it. We aren't told how long he lived with the bewildering dilemma. It must have been an enormous strain on him personally, let alone the effect it could have on his livelihood and standing in the community.

Although his decision to work out a quiet separation is the best solution he could figure out, it didn't seem to be motivated primarily by self-interest. Scripture says he arrived at it because he was a righteous man and didn't want to subject Mary to disgrace. He loved her that much.

When Joseph thinks seriously about this course of action, God intervenes. An angel speaks to Joseph in a dream. This isn't a dream filled with symbolism and requiring interpretation. The angel addresses Joseph by name and refers to Mary by name. He tells him not to be afraid of taking Mary as his wife and explains that the Holy Spirit is responsible for her conception.

The angel goes so far as to tell him he should name the child Jesus. This showed a trust in Joseph that he would follow through, since naming a child didn't take place until eight days after birth. We know that when Joseph wakes up he doesn't hesitate to continue the next steps of marriage and take Mary as his wife (v. 24). Now that the couple are certain individually of a divine plan in motion, they can live the wonder-filled adventure together. It won't be easy, but together they will rest in the Wonder-Worker's promise and power. He is with them.

———————

To ponder:

In our seasons of dilemma, we are not alone. God's promises are true. His power is working.

M – *Mem*

*'Your commandments give me understanding; no wonder I hate
every false way of life' (v. 104, NLT).*

The next octave of verses from Psalm 119 reminds us that God's Word
gives us wisdom and understanding. The written word of God and the
Living Word of God, Christ, are in accord.

Studying the written word helps us to know the one the New Testament
calls the Word (*logos*). In the first chapter of John's Gospel, even before
John tells us his name in verse 17, he refers to Jesus as the Word (verses 1
and 14). Later, in the opening of Revelation, John says he's been exiled
because of his witness to the word of God, the testimony of Jesus (1:9).
Near the end of the book the conquering Christ is called 'the Word of God'
(19:13). John uses the term without explanation because it is a familiar
theological expression in his day.

With this in mind, we read today's passage. The word and the Word give
wisdom and understanding to those who keep them as constant
companions and continue to obey them. The psalmist's testimony that
God's Word makes him wiser than his enemies, could have been the
prophet Daniel's testimony as well. Both recognise the source of their
wisdom. Perhaps that is why the psalmist can delight that he has more
insight than his teachers and more understanding than his elders.

He is not flaunting his knowledge nor adopting a relative or subjective
view of truth, as postmodernism does today. Nevertheless John Wesley
cautions: 'So you ascribe all the knowledge you have to God; and in this
respect you are humble. But if you think you have more than you really
have, or if you think you're so taught of God, as no longer to need man's
teaching; pride lieth at the door.'[22]

The emphasis in verse 102 is not that the writer is self-sufficient or the
ideal pupil, but that God is a great teacher. The psalmist realises that God's
Word holds high personal and practical value. If we do as well, how can we
animate that truth today?

Richly Graced

'And Mary said, "My soul magnifies and extols the Lord, And my spirit rejoices in God my Saviour"' (vv. 46, 47, AB).

When Gabriel first greets Mary he calls her a highly favoured one and assures her that the Lord is with her (v. 28). It's not that she is particularly deserving, but God-blessed. True, the way Mary is graced carries unique privilege as the only one in history to bear the Messiah. But, as believers, we are also favoured for the role God has for us. Paul writes in Ephesians 1:2–6 that we are chosen to be holy and blameless before God through Christ, to bring praise to his freely given grace. God looks for those through whom his grace can flow.

Mary's life may have seemed obscure or ordinary, yet God knew her and her situation. So, too, every person is important to God. In spite of being humanly unreasonable, God's choice of Mary reminds us that nothing is impossible with God. And her response tells us that God honours faith in him.

Scripture tells us that at times Mary pondered events. Perhaps she shared the contemplative nature of another Mary, Martha's sister. By the time Mary arrives in the hill country to visit Elizabeth, she has had plenty of time to mull over the angel's announcement.

We might not normally expect the elderly cousin to be so animated or the youthful one so reflective. In response to Elizabeth's surprising greeting, and possibly relieved to have someone with whom to share her news, from a full heart Mary freely pours out praise to God. Some call it the Magnificat, others Mary's song.

Her song has several stanzas. It reveals an awareness of covenant promises and their fulfilment through her Child. First, as Hannah did in the Old Testament (1 Samuel 2), Mary praises God and rejoices in him for the special blessing he's brought to her. She can't literally magnify God. No one can add anything to him. But her praise honours him and draws attention to his greatness. Does our worship do that too?

Mary's Song (1)

'His mercy extends to those who fear him, from generation to generation'
(v. 50).

After rejoicing in her Saviour for his grace to her, Mary continues her beautiful song. She describes the Lord as faithful, powerful, holy and merciful. When Mary declares the ways in which God, through his Messiah, will rectify the wrongs in the world, it becomes a hopeful song. People will be surprised at the Messiah's radical, innovative approach. The God-way will overturn traditional assumptions.

William Barclay says: 'There is loveliness in the Magnificat but in that loveliness there is dynamite. Christianity begets a revolution in each man and revolution in the world.'[23]

Transformation begins with change in individuals. Christ's life and message address human pride (v. 51). He teaches new ways of seeing. He doesn't let us get away with measuring ourselves by our own standards or by what others think of us. His holy light shines into our inner thoughts and we see ourselves as we are. Since it's contrary to human nature, we know we need divine aid if we are to be willing to love our enemies and forgive freely.

Transformation naturally moves from individuals to society. When Mary's song says the Messiah casts down those in seats of power (v. 52) and exalts the humble, it implies that Christ comes for all people, especially those not thought powerful. He redefines the kingdom of God by welcoming those whom society excludes. Some of the 'humble' of his day whom Jesus exalted were children, women and people of other races.

Christ's underlying appeal to value every person regardless of status continues to require attention in society and by each of us.

———————

To ponder:

What part do I play in helping the Church reflect Christ's programme globally as well as locally in my generation?

Mary's Song (2)

'Sing to the LORD a new song, for he has done marvellous things; his right hand and his holy arm have worked salvation for him . . . He has remembered his love and his faithfulness to the house of Israel; all the ends of the earth have seen the salvation of our God' (Psalm 98:1, 3).

Mary's song also features a Saviour who fills the hungry, but sends the rich away (v. 53). We think of the beatitude about being filled if we hunger for righteousness, but Jesus fed people who needed tangible food too. He often spoke about money and possessions.

Jesus taught that we receive, not to amass but to give as freely as we have received. It's a radical shift in how we view what is ours. A motive of love supplants the usual motive of greed. Security isn't chiefly in our assets but in God and in the interdependent believing community that responds to his direction.

Nicholas was a Christian of the fourth century who lived in what is today Turkey. At an early age he received a sizeable inheritance when his parents died. Nicholas dedicated his life to serving God and was generous with his wealth – using it all to help the sick and needy, often anonymously.

He became Bishop of Myra at an early age and was imprisoned for his faith. Later he attended the Council of Nicea. Nicholas died on 6 December 343. The anniversary of his death became St Nicholas Day, still observed in some countries today. The day's modest gift-giving in early December sometimes helps preserve a focus on Christ on Christmas Day.

Perhaps as Mary finishes her divinely inspired spontaneous song she remembers Scripture she's learned by heart. The Old Testament is full of references to God's faithfulness to his promises to Israel (see our key verse). She praises God for showing Israel special favour through the coming Child. God was mercifully fulfilling his covenant promise to Abraham and his descendants (vv. 54, 55).

Mary's Way

*'Let the word of Christ dwell in you richly, in all wisdom, teaching and
admonishing each other, in psalms, and hymns, and spiritual songs,
in grace singing in your hearts to the Lord' (Colossians 3:16, YLT).*

From what we've noticed about Mary, what might the way she handled
the announcement and miracle God sent her teach us? Perhaps we'd
take counsel to be alert, be willing, be grateful or be careful. But miracles
take time and we need to know how to sustain watchful obedience. Mary's
took nine months. In his book, *The Mary Miracle*, Jack Hayford suggests
that we keep a spirit of surrender, faith and submission while we wait for
God's plan to unfold by noting the Mary way of handling miracles.

First he says: 'The Mary way to respond to a miracle promise begun in
your life is to find how you can serve the miracle God is working in
someone else.'[24] The angel didn't suggest that Mary visit Elizabeth, but
Mary did and she stayed three months with her older relative. Mary
probably assisted Elizabeth in practical ways. Mary no doubt benefited
from the counsel and experience of an older woman of faith. Serving
someone else's miracle benefits both them and us.

Another lesson from Mary's example is the importance of songs of faith
in keeping us steady through the interim of waiting. Sing or read faith-
affirming words from a songbook or hymnal. Turn to the psalms often.
Listen to music that focuses on the Lord. Try writing a song even if only
to sing privately to the Lord. There's a connection in our key verse between
singing with grateful hearts to God and the word of Christ dwelling in us
richly.

Finally, we don't notice Mary trying to explain what's happening, figure
it all out or defend herself. She exhibited a simple trust in God. He took
care to bring Joseph to understanding and acceptance. God took care of
announcing Christ's birth to the shepherds and moving the magi to search
for him. As time went on and the miracle unfolded, more became clear. As
we wait, we too can serve others; sing to the Lord and let God work.

God's Hand with Him

'Everyone who heard this wondered about it, asking, "What then is this child going to be?" For the Lord's hand was with him' (v. 66).

The arrival of a baby was a double blessing to Zechariah and Elizabeth. That their heir was a boy was especially welcome news in Jewish circles, as it still is in some cultures today. Jewish law said that baby boys should be circumcised on their eighth day of life. We note the couple's obedient compliance. No doubt traditional music and rejoicing add to the festive event. Friends gather to offer congratulations and be present for the naming.

But when the consensus is to name the child after his father, Elizabeth protests. She is definite. His name should be John. The crowd of well-wishers objects. There is no John in the baby's family.

The neighbours appeal to mute Zechariah to counter the mother's notions. He calls for what he's relied on to communicate for nearly a year – a tablet (probably covered with wax). The onlookers watch as he writes: 'His name is John' (v. 63).

Then Zechariah starts to talk! He begins by praising God. Now the buzz isn't just the boy's unlikely name, but the father's ability to speak again. They wonder what it means and what unique divine calling the child will have. Years later when John begins to preach, some may remember this day. Zechariah's obedience to God's message – 'Call him John' – not only brings his own restoration, but is a practical witness to others.

Scripture says that from the outset the hand of the Lord was with John. A similar phrase was used of two notable Old Testament prophets – Elijah and Elisha. In the days of the Early Church, when Christians scattered from Jerusalem they spread the gospel to Jews wherever they went. But believers from Cyrene and Cyprus spread the gospel to Greeks in Antioch. Of these unnamed Christians who dared to share the good news with Gentiles, it was said: 'The Lord's hand was with them, and a great number of people believed and turned to the Lord' (Acts 11:21).

To ponder:

Where do we see 'the Lord's hand' today?

All the Days of My Life

'To enable us to serve him without fear in holiness and righteousness before him all our days' (vv. 74, 75).

After a single verse stating John's birth, and several more describing the events on his naming day, under the inspiration of the Holy Spirit the child's father prophesises in what is sometimes called Zechariah's Song or *Benedictus*. If it reminds us of some psalms, it could be because Zechariah had been steeped in Hebrew Scriptures for decades. Since most priests began their ministry at the age of thirty, Zechariah had probably been a priest for a long time. Through his song, for a brief time Zechariah is also a prophet. But John's entire ministry would be that of an extraordinary prophet.

Zechariah starts by praising God for visiting his people, redeeming them and raising a Saviour through David's line. As often happens in prophecies, Zechariah speaks as if things that are yet to come have already come to pass. That's how certain he is that God's plans are being fulfilled.

The enemies that Zechariah says God delivers from might in his mind relate to the social and political oppressors of Israel in his day, but they have a greater implication. Christ came to deliver us from the greatest enemies of humanity – sin and Satan.

Zechariah folds the Old Testament prophets, prophecies and covenant into his song. He unequivocally declares the purpose of God's deliverance is enabling people to live to serve the Lord fearlessly in holiness and righteousness.

If we could have handed him a Salvation Army flag, this would have been the time he would have waved it, since it also symbolises the gospel by reminding us of God's loving offer of deliverance and holiness: red for Christ's blood on the cross for our redemption; blue for the purity of God and challenge to holy living; yellow for the fire of the Holy Spirit, agent of our cleansing and keeping as we obediently respond to the Lord. Such inward grace is not only meant for future heavenly realms, but for our day-by-day living.

N – *Nun*

'My heart is set on keeping your decrees to the very end' (v. 112).

The tenor of the previous section of Psalm 119 was indeed delight. The psalmist even compared God's Word to the sweetness of honey (v. 103). In today's section he starts with an upbeat declaration to the Lord: 'By your words I can see where I'm going; they throw a beam of light on my dark path, (v. 105, *MSG*).

If there's a power cut at night, we can manage to get around by candlelight for a while, but we're relieved when the power is restored, or daylight comes, and we can move more freely and get on with our lives. The psalmist sees God's Word as giving immediate short-range and ongoing long-range light. It gives us guidance for our day-to-day walk, our step-by-step way through difficult times and our lifelong journey through life.

The psalmist will end the section with determination, but the tone of several intervening verses (107, 109 and 110) is not rosy. The dark paths the psalmist realistically mentions include suffering, life's hazards and danger from enemies. Each time what steadies him is God's Word. He relies on God to keep his promises; he purposes to remember God's Word and to stay aligned with it as he has vowed.

The poet asks God to accept the willing praise of his mouth (v. 108) – another version says the freewill offerings of his mouth. These could have been in contrast to the fixed offerings ritual required. The Septuagint offers the alternative, 'what I say spontaneously'.

In the same spirit of spontaneity, in the New Testament we're reminded: 'Through Jesus, therefore, let us continually offer to God a sacrifice of praise – the fruit of lips that confess his name' (Hebrews 13:15).

In one of his hymns (*SASB* 7) Horatius Bonar details his desire for praise to be present in his daily living and outlook, and prays for 'a life made up of praise in every part'. In addition to our good intentions, if we ask for the Spirit's help and continue to depend on the Word, praise will rise.

In His Light

'For with you is the fountain of life; in your light we see light' (Psalm 36:9).

If Zechariah's song was a symphonic poem, the piece might open with bold, deliberate music. But the final four verses would slow down and, as the notes die away, portray a more pensive ending. When Zechariah turns from the grand themes of his inspired song to address his son personally, he doesn't speak as a parent, but continues as a prophet. Although he both foretells and tells forth John's role, the focus remains on Christ.

John is born for a unique mission. As the Messiah's forerunner, he would be known as the prophet of the Most High. Strangely, some confused Jesus with John. Jesus said that John was more than a prophet since he was the one whom God promised in Malachi to send ahead of Messiah's coming. Jesus spoke of John as the predicted 'Elijah' who would precede the Messiah.

John's mission of preparation would involve waking people up to their need for salvation and God's provision for it, then calling them to seek God's forgiveness through repentance of sins. In a sense, John's mission remains the spiritual mission of all Christian ministers who point people to Christ.

In verse 78 Zechariah echoes Malachi 4:2 ('sun of righteousness') when he says that in God's mercy, the rising sun ['the Dayspring' (*NKJV*) or 'the first light of Heaven' (*JBP*)] will visit us to dispel the darkness of mankind. The apostle John says that John the Baptist was a witness concerning that true light, Christ (John 1:4–9). Once the light of God comes and offsets death's shadow, then he shows us the way to peace, step by step (Luke 1:79).

In 'O come, O come, Emmanuel', when we sing: 'O come, thou Dayspring, come and cheer our spirits by thine advent here', not only do we use a tune from the fifteenth century and words of prayer from the twelfth, but we refer to Christ as Zechariah and Malachi did centuries before. He is ever the Light of the world.

The Long-Promised Saviour Comes

'But when the proper time had fully come, God sent His Son, born of a woman' (Galatians 4:4, AB).

We aren't certain if the registration noted in Luke 2:1 was for census or taxation purposes or both. It was a Roman decree. The census could ascertain the number of males available for military duty. But at that time in Palestine, Jews were exempt from the military.

Some commentators tell us the custom of going back to the town of one's ancestral roots was by Jewish preference. Roman custom would be to register where one lived. Neither Roman nor Jewish law required women to accompany the men for the registration. So, under the guidance of the Holy Spirit, Joseph chose to go to Bethlehem and Mary chose to go the eighty miles with him.

Today, in some countries, a child born by 31 December can be taken as a tax deduction that year. We don't know whether it was an asset or liability to list a child for the Roman census in Jesus' day. At least Mary and Joseph weren't any more surprised than Elizabeth and Zechariah had been when their baby was a boy. Since Jesus was born at census time, he no doubt became a statistic, one more male child born to David's line.

Most details surrounding Christ's birth remain a mystery. We can only speculate about Mary's labour, attendants, comfort or delivery. We aren't sure if the word translated 'manger' meant a feeding trough or a stable. In those days it was the custom for local minstrels who heard that a birth was imminent, if the child turned out to be a boy, to play and sing in welcoming celebration.

Mary and Joseph may have missed hearing such a happy sound. But not far from Bethlehem, others rejoiced at the announcement. And through the words of hymnwriter Philip Doddridge, at the news of the long-promised Saviour's coming we sing:

> Let every heart prepare a throne,
> And every voice a song.
>
> (*SASB* 81)

Candid Evangelists

'They spread the word concerning what had been told them about this child'
(v. 17).

The world-changing divine news was announced to people whose occupation meant they lived with and tended animals. Although a traditional occupation, shepherding was regarded by Jews as ordinary and lowly. God's choice of recipients of his good news tells us something about how he views people. No one is too insignificant or common for his interest.

Flocks for the temple were tended near Bethlehem, so it may have been to shepherds overseeing sheep destined for sacrifice that the angel announced the birth of the Lamb of God that night. When joined by a great company of angels (some translations say a heavenly army, knighthood or soldiers) their praises would have exceeded any celebration a local minstrel band could have mustered on the occasion of a birth.

The first news of the Messiah's coming came to very ordinary people – a carpenter and his wife. Earlier Gabriel alluded to the event when he spoke to Zechariah. Even he was not a prominent person, merely of the rank and file of 20,000 priests. Now the message comes to shepherds, carrying on a profession older than that of the priests.

We wonder how these down-to-earth people felt about being the recipients of such unearthly news and in such dramatic style. The Lord knows he can count on them to look for the newborn Christ in the city of David, Bethlehem. When the angels leave and the shepherds can converse, their focus is on getting to town, probably their own city, to see proof of the message for themselves.

They don't doubt it has happened (v. 15). The details help. A child in a manger is unusual and might be more easily found. Further, such a humble setting won't intimidate them. They're eager to be off. And once they've found the Christ, they're eager to confidently tell everyone the whole story of the astonishing news. Uplifted, they return to work with full hearts, still praising God.

Temple Visit

'It's now out in the open for everyone to see' (v. 31, MSG).

According to Jewish custom, a baby boy is circumcised and named eight days after birth, as Elizabeth and Zechariah did with John. Mary and Joseph observe Mosaic law and Jewish customs as well. As far as we know, other than Mary and Joseph, no one knows of the name – Jesus – until that day. We aren't told of any opposition to their choice of the name, possibly because they aren't in their home town or surrounded by friends and family.

About a month later the family travels to Jerusalem for further Jewish rites. They want to follow the command to present their firstborn to the Lord (see Exodus 13). But first, according to Leviticus 12, Mary needs to present a sacrifice for her purification – a lamb and a dove. Those who can't afford to offer both are permitted to offer two doves, or even as little as some flour. People actually only bring the price of the animals to the temple. Mary drops her payment for doves into a trumpet-shaped coffer in the court of the women, and then is sprinkled by the blood of the sacrificed doves.

Besides the ritual for Mary, the couple must present their firstborn to God in token of his claim to the child and his service. They probably do both in the outer court – near the temple's East Gate, the main entrance. No doubt Zechariah and Elizabeth had done the same six months before, when we can imagine Zechariah's awe at returning to the place of his encounter with the angel.

It is likely that the elderly widow Anna, who practically lives at the temple, is there on both of Zechariah's visits; possibly Simeon is as well. Now, in the prophetic tradition, when the righteous, Spirit-led man meets Jesus' family, he rejoices in the fulfilment of God's promises to bring salvation to Israel and the Gentiles.

Since Simeon's life's longing is fulfilled, he is ready to be released from life. He gives the parents a blessing and a stark prediction. Then, despite sorrow and ageing, Anna's prayerful, worshipful presence and her open testimony about the Messiah hearten them.

Thank God for the Simeons and Annas in the Church today!

Christmas Songs

'Sing to the LORD a new song; sing to the LORD, all the earth' (v. 1).

Elizabeth broke into a song of blessing when she saw her cousin. Mary sang of the goodness of the Lord and the rightness of his way. Zechariah sang a benediction over his son, John.

The angel's extraordinary announcement to the shepherds and the angelic host's refrain, whether proclaimed or sung, made a memorable choral presentation. The shepherds could repeat it to Mary and Joseph. Then the shepherds didn't hesitate to broadly spread word of Christ's birth. They returned from Bethlehem full of ceaseless praise to God for what they'd heard from the angels and seen for themselves to be true.

Forty days later, at Jesus' dedication in the temple, came what some call the 'Canticle of Simeon'. It is still sung in evening services in some churches. Salvation Army songwriter Keith Banks weds Simeon's prayer with a lingering melody in his 'Simeon's Song':

> Lord, you have kept your promise,
> Now let your servant go in peace.
> Lord, you have kept your promise,
> Now let your servant go in peace.
>
> With my own eyes, with my own eyes
> I have seen thy salvation;
> With my own eyes, with my own eyes,
> I have seen the Lord.[25]

This is the thirtieth anniversary year of The Salvation Army's International Staff Songsters (ISS). When the group was re-formed in 1980, General Arnold Brown observed: 'I hope none of us will forget that the very first word sung by the ISS was the word "Jesus".' As we sing the songs of Christmas, traditional or new, let us consider Jesus, the one who gives the heart a song and is the reason we sing.

Tradition

'But whoever lives by the truth comes into the light, so that it may be seen plainly that what he has done has been done through God' (v. 21).

In the documentary film *God Grew Tired of Us*, five young men, battered and displaced by civil war in Sudan, move to America where they face unexpected challenges in coping with the foreign culture. From everyday skills for city living and adjusting to unfamiliar foods and products to language issues and significantly different weather, everything tests them.

They survive together in an apartment. Among other initial impressions, they find Christmas traditions puzzling. Amid the months of decorations and advertisements, little reminds them of the Christmas they knew in Sudan, where Christians gathered to celebrate by focusing on the birth of Christ.

We can understand their confusion, since so many of the traditions we enjoy at Christmas sprang up within the context of culture or have been adapted and accommodated into forms our forebears would hardly recognise. The secular world is sometimes willing to accept a charming Bethlehem scene as part of the season's trappings. Babies can be disarming.

But faith based on the facts of the incarnation can see beyond Bethlehem to the redemption, resurrection and reconciliation God offers through Christ. As helpful as traditions can be, perhaps we need to assess some of them in the radiant reality of Scripture instead of the glitziness of television advertisements; to unwrap what our culture has folded into the season; to go beyond a greeting-card understanding.

Those who have lived outside their own country at Christmas often find that there can be a wonderful simplicity in rediscovering, as if for the first time, that the essence of Christmas celebration really is the Christmas story. But we don't have to leave home to be intentional about reflecting and marvelling at Emmanuel's coming. Then we can embrace the traditions that symbolise our joy and possibly discover new ones that honour the Lord.

S – Samech

*'The Life-Light blazed out of the darkness; the darkness couldn't
put it out' (John 1:5, MSG).*

In today's segment of Psalm 119 the writer sharply contrasts two ways –
the way of life and the way of death. He doesn't try to be politically
correct. The psalmist clearly finds solace in God's Word. Standing against
the double-minded, evildoers, hope-dashers, deceitful drifters and wicked
he's encountered, the psalmist calls God's Word his sole stability, his
refuge, his life support and his hope for justice. He cherishes what God
says and he relies on God's terrifying yet grand judgement to be sure and
right.

On this Christmas Sunday, or in the final days before Christmas, some
of us will participate in candlelight services. It will likely be a reflective,
peaceful time. Typically, we will sing 'Silent Night' in a dimmed chapel, as
many hold candles.

An elderly Japanese woman told me of one of her most precious
memories from her youth. Although war had curtailed electricity, in
December Christians in Tokyo gathered to celebrate the birth of Christ.
She was deeply moved when by candlelight they sang the words of Joseph
Mohr's popular carol:

> Silent night! Holy night!
> Son of God, love's pure light,
> Radiant beams from thy holy face,
> With the dawn of redeeming grace,
> Jesus, Lord, at thy birth.

In wonder, we again consider Christ, the Light of the world, who came into
the darkness of humankind to bring us hope; entered the darkness of our
sin to bring us redemption. The contrasts, as in today's portion of psalm,
are great. We rejoice with John in his description: 'In him appeared life and
this life was the light of mankind. The light still shines in the darkness and
the darkness has never put it out' (John 1:4, 5, *JBP*). Hallelujah!

Deck the Halls with . . .

'I am the gate; whoever enters through me will be saved' (John 10:9).

What traditions are essential to your Christmas celebration – a tree, sprigs of evergreen, a manger, an Advent wreath, children's pageants, concerts, gifts, Advent readings, charitable gifts, Christmas cards, special foods, sounds of bells or carols, candles, Chrismons or Christingles? The last two, although new to us, have been meaningful Christmas traditions for others for decades.

Fifty years ago a woman originated Chrismons[26] for her Lutheran church in Virginia, USA. They are white and gold Christmas tree decorations used in churches and homes of Christians. When they are handmade by a small group there is opportunity for discussion about the meaning behind emblems of Christian faith. There are typical Christmas shapes as might be seen on church banners – the manger, angels, star and wise men, candles and other symbols suggesting events in Jesus' life and ministry or titles of Christ.

Created in the eighteenth century, the Christingle (or 'Christ Light') helps children understand the meaning of Christmas. In the first Christingle service a Moravian pastor gave each child a lighted candle wrapped in a red ribbon with a prayer that said: 'Lord Jesus, kindle a flame in these dear children's hearts.' The Children's Society, which used Christingles as fundraisers, introduced them to churches in England, where Christingle celebrations have become popular during Advent and Epiphany.

Today's Christingle is an orange (the world), encircled by a red ribbon (the blood of Christ), decorated with fruits and sweets (fruits of the earth) skewered into the orange on four sticks (north, south, east and west). A lighted candle (Christ) is inserted into the centre of the orange, which becomes its holder.

God used visual prompts to remind his people of their connection to him and his word. Jesus used everyday word pictures to help people visualise and remember his teaching (for example John 10:7–9). How does what we display at Christmas honour the Lord and his word?

That Date

'Behold, now is truly the time for a gracious welcome and acceptance [of you from God]; behold, now is the day of salvation!' (v. 2, AB).

The Christian year begins with Advent even as the calendar year winds down. Consider Salvation Army poet Flora Larsson's prayer poem, and then pray that someone you know will welcome new life in Christ this Christmas:

'What's the Date?'

You made quite a local impact, Master,
when as a babe you joined the human race in Bethlehem.
Wondrous tales abound of stars, angels, shepherds and wise men
all accompanying your advent.
Many people do not believe that story.
They scoff at the Christmas gospel
while enjoying Christmas festivities.
But while they scoff, they acknowledge you,
You who they say never existed.
Every time they say: 'What's the date?'
they are asking: 'When was Jesus born?'
Each time they date a letter, they pay silent homage to your coming.
Before Christ and After Christ . . . so is history divided.
BC and AD – Anno Domini – Year of our Lord.

Master, I pray at this festive season that someone
who has lived quite factually
'before Christ' in their lives
will take the personal decisive step into AD,
Year of our Lord,
acknowledging you as Saviour and King.[27]

In Christ

'For God was in Christ, reconciling the world to himself' (v. 19, NLT).

We look down from the window of an aircraft or tall building and think we see the toy-like cars and ant-like people as God does. But it's really only a bird's-eye view. God's view of his creation is not remote. As the song 'Someone Cares' puts it:

> Ours is not a distant God, remote, unfeeling,
> Who is careless of our loneliness and pain.
> *John Gowans* (*SASB* 238)

In Christ, God became as one of us and conversed with people face to face. Through his incarnation, he was with us. Through Christ's sacrificial death, he was for us. By his Holy Spirit, he comes to live in us and through us.

Using the well-known Christmas tune to which we sing 'Christians, awake', try the refreshing words by Salvation Army poet and songwriter, Retired General John Gowans (based on 2 Corinthians 5:19). Delight in the truth of our incarnate Lord's redemptive and transformative power:

> *God was in Christ*
>
> God was in Christ. The miracle is true!
> God was in man a wonder-work to do.
> There to be close, the human and divine.
> Sharing one body like your own, and mine.
> Showing to us what God alone can do,
> Once he has come to live in me, in you!
>
> God is in me, inside my head, my heart.
> He lives in me, at home in ev'ry part;
> Opened my mind, his purpose to fulfil,
> Sharing one object and one common will,
> Making it plain what I can do and be
> Now he has come to live in me. In me!

What Child is This?

'In him was life, and that life was the light of men' (v. 4).

A Christmas presentation is titled *It Began in Bethlehem*. Scripture tells us where Jesus was born and that his human life began in Mary's womb but, unlike us, that was not his beginning: 'In the beginning the Word already existed. The Word was with God, and the Word was God' (v. 1, *NLT*). He is God. As part of the Trinity, Jesus had no beginning. Jesus claimed both pre-existence and Godhood (John 8:58).

Joseph and Mary were separately instructed by an angel to name the divine child Jesus – a form of the Hebrew name Joshua, or 'God will save us'. He is the Saviour. He is the one chosen to bring humankind salvation.

He comes to live among us and show us the Father: 'The Word became flesh and made his dwelling among us. We have seen his glory, the glory of the One and Only, who came from the Father, full of grace and truth' (1:14). He is the anointed one, the Christ.

When the wise men seek the Christ in Jerusalem, they ask for the child born 'King of the Jews'. The appellation disturbs King Herod who determines to kill the infant king. Later, one of the disciples calls Jesus 'King of Israel' (John 1:49) the first time they meet.

During Jesus' ministry when he used parables to teach about the kingdom or coming judgement, he used veiled references to himself as King. On Palm Sunday, he did not rebuke those who hailed him as King, although the disciples didn't realise the full import of that day until he had risen. He is the King.

When Pilate asked the Lord if he was the King of the Jews, Jesus said that he was. Perhaps that prompted Pilate to fix a sign to the cross, 'Jesus of Nazareth, King of the Jews' (John 19:19). Because of Christ's obedience, 'God exalted him to the highest place and gave him the name that is above every name, that at the name of Jesus every knee should bow . . . and every tongue confess that Jesus Christ is Lord, to the glory of God the Father' (Philippians 2:9–11). Amen!

Nailed to Earth for Me

'But Mary kept all these things, and pondered them in her heart' (2:19 KJV).

We know that from the outset Mary magnified the Lord. In her poem *Mary's Song*, poet Luci Shaw considers what the new mother might have pondered:

> Blue homespun and the bend of my breast
> keep warm this small hot naked star
> fallen to my arms. (Rest . . .
> you who have had so far
> to come.) Now nearness satisfies
> the body of God sweetly. Quiet he lies
> whose vigour hurled
> a universe. He sleeps
> whose eyelids have not closed before.
> His breath (so slight it seems
> no breath at all) once ruffled the dark deeps
> to sprout a world.
> Charmed by doves' voices, the whisper of straw,
> he dreams,
> hearing no music from his other spheres.
> Breath, mouth, ears, eyes
> he is curtailed
> who overflowed all skies,
> all years.
> Older than eternity, now he
> is new. Now native to earth as I am, nailed
> to my poor planet, caught that I might be free,
> blind in my womb to know my darkness ended,
> brought to this birth
> for me to be new-born,
> and for him to see me mended
> I must see him torn.[28]

Christmas

*'So the Word became human and made his home among us. He was
full of unfailing love and faithfulness. And we have seen his glory,
the glory of the Father's one and only Son' (v.14, NLT).*

On this Christmas Day, may you know the joy, peace and hope that
Christ brings each upturned heart. Before we sleep on this busy,
happy day, perhaps we will follow the poet's advice to 'Linger at the
Manger':

Linger at the manger on this holy night of nights,
Gaze upon the beauty of God's Son, the Light of lights.
Sense the wonder and the joy this sacred moment brings,
Listen to the lullaby the virgin mother sings.
Contemplate the mystery of God enrobed in flesh:
Linger at the manger for a while.

Linger at the manger with the wise men from afar,
Led to Bethl'em's stable by the brightness of a star.
See the precious gifts they offer to the holy Child
As they kneel in rev'rence to the Baby, meek and mild.
Bow your heart and head with them, and worship Christ, the King:
Linger at the manger for a while.

Linger at the manger with the shepherds; hear them tell
How God's only Son has come to earth, with us to dwell,
Heralded by angels singing in the midnight sky,
Telling of a Saviour who has come to live and die.
Think that here before you lies the perfect Lamb of God:
Linger at the manger for a while.

Robert E. Thomson
(Commissioner Thomson lives in retirement in the USA)

A – *Ayin*

*'But when the kindness and love of God our Saviour appeared, he saved us,
not because of righteous things we had done, but because of his mercy.
He saved us through the washing of rebirth and renewal by the Holy Spirit,
whom he poured out on us generously through Jesus Christ our Saviour,
so that, having been justified by his grace, we might become heirs having
the hope of eternal life' (Titus 3:4–7).*

At first the psalmist may appear to be declaring his own merits, not unlike today when someone claims they try to be a good person, do the right things and give to good causes in hope of tipping the scales of divine judgement in their favour.

There are many ways people try to merit divine favour. Some follow prescribed rituals. Others vow to try harder to do better or bargain with God. In some cultures, the end of the calendar year obliges people to settle outstanding debts and clear out unwanted belongings. Some feel compelled to give to the poor. In Japan, on top of that, those who visit a Buddhist temple on New Year's Eve participate in ringing an enormous bell 108 times to dispel the sins common to humankind – if only temporarily.

Even the Jewish practice of animal sacrifice was not a permanent solution. But we know that Jesus Christ, the Lamb of God, came to pay for our sins and cleanse us. Confession of sin and faith in his redeeming power puts us right with God. Good deeds should flow out of a forgiven life, but can never offset God's one-sided grace.

In verse 123 the psalmist clarifies that he's longingly looking for the divine salvation God has promised. The next two verses show that not only does the writer have a teachable spirit, but also that he wants to be dealt with according to God's love.

In the next breath he tells the Lord it's time for him to do something about those who flagrantly disobey his word. We may be surprised at his boldness but recognise its source. The psalmist loves God's Word more than pure gold and counts on it being the standard of righteousness applied to all – and so may we.

More Questions

*'They asked around, "Where can we find and pay homage
to the newborn King of the Jews?" ' (v. 2, MSG).*

Truth and faith need not be rivals. Francis Collins, doctor, author,
scientist and former director of the Human Genome Research Project
which oversaw the deciphering and sequencing of DNA, is an evangelical
Christian. In 2009 he launched the BioLogos Foundation to promote the
search for truth in both the natural and spiritual realms and harmony
between these perspectives.

The magi or wise men Matthew describes may be from the scholarly
class of an Eastern region such as Arabia, Mesopotamia or Persia. As such
they are educated in philosophy, natural science, medicine and religion.
Rulers count on their advice. Although the order of the magi will deterio-
rate later, around the time of Christ's birth it is at its best and consists of
good, holy men who seek truth.

From their study they have some inkling that a king of the Jews will be
born. Roman historians of the time write about a growing general expectation that a new world leader would soon emerge. Seeing a particularly
brilliant star in their homeland greatly impresses the wise men. They link it
with the royal birth. They may have many questions, but their quest is no
quixotic whim. They are so certain that something significant has
happened that they undertake a lengthy journey.

The wise men logically assume that they'll find a ruler in the capital city.
Perhaps they also hope to find an interpreter there. They do discover
further details in Jerusalem, some helpful and some troubling. The
Messiah's birthplace is foretold as Bethlehem. That he may have been born
at all agitates the king and troubles the city. The citizens who know Herod's
treachery know it doesn't bode well for them if a rival is at hand, even as a
baby.

If the seekers lose sight of the star while with Herod and the scholars in
Jerusalem, as they resume their trip and see it leading them again, their
sense of divine guidance returns (v. 9).

Seek, Find, Worship

*'They entered the house and saw the child in the arms of Mary, his mother.
Overcome, they kneeled and worshipped him. Then they opened their
luggage and presented gifts: gold, frankincense, myrrh' (v. 11, MSG).*

Sincere seekers for truth find it. The men who come a long way looking
for Christ find him. The non-Jewish wise men are led by God to Christ
the King. They are the first Gentiles to look to him and are first-fruits of
all of us who turn to God for salvation through Christ.

Earlier, the shepherds went to verify what the angel told them about the
Saviour's birth. Then they spread the word and glorified God on the way
back to their fields. Perhaps they also worshipped at the manger, but we
aren't told. On the other hand, the wise men's immediate response when
they discover Christ is obeisance, worship and offering him gifts. We, the
shepherds and kings of today, can approach him verifying and testifying as
well as adoring, worshipping and giving.

We don't know how many wise men there were, but the three gifts
traditionally suggest three givers. Besides gold – fitting for a king and even
today of lasting value – they give frankincense, suitable for a priest since it
is used in worship. Priests sprinkle it on certain sacrifices and burn it
during prayers. The scent of sacrifice and prayer lingers. Although
undetected by the saturated pray-er, others readily detect it.

Since it is used to embalm bodies, myrrh is the gift fit for one who has
died. Thirty-three years later, women repeat this symbolic gift. First one
anoints Jesus with her fragrant oil which Jesus says she uses in preparation
for his burial (John 12:7); and then several come to his tomb sadly bearing
the weight of burial spices but are liberated as the first witnesses of Christ's
resurrection (Mark 16, Matthew 28).

William Barclay rightly says that these gifts foretold that Christ 'was to
be the true King, the perfect High Priest, and in the end the supreme
Saviour of men'.[29] Hallelujah!

Safely Led

'Joseph was directed in a dream to go to the hills of Galilee' (v. 22, MSG).

Herod started his career decades before as governor of the region. But when Jesus is born in Bethlehem, Herod is the entrenched king of Judea. He keeps the peace, constructs impressive buildings and in difficult times can be generous enough to rescind taxes. Yet he is a suspicious ruler who even puts his wife, mother-in-law and three of his sons to death when he thinks they might usurp his power. He only gets worse as he ages.

No wonder he is worried when the wise men arrive with news of a child destined to be king in his region. He wastes no time in investigating with Jewish religious scholars and aristocracy. Armed with the latest reports, he privately gives deceitful direction to the visitors. Herod says they should diligently seek out the child and report back so he also can worship him. But he plans to get rid of the potential rival.

Joseph isn't noted in the scene when the magi visit Bethlehem. The wise men are warned in a dream and judiciously go home by a route that keeps them out of Herod's sight. It doesn't take the king long to discover he's been tricked. He won't be outwitted: he'll have all boy toddlers in the vicinity of Bethlehem killed. Yet no one will stop God's plan to redeem his world.

Now Joseph takes centre stage. For the second time an angel appears to Joseph in a dream. He's to take his family to Egypt and stay there until further notice because Herod wants to kill Jesus. The family stays in Egypt until, through another dream, Joseph is told to return to Israel because the tyrant is dead (vv. 19, 20). No doubt they mean to return to Bethlehem, but another dream combines with Joseph's dread of the new king – Herod's son. So Joseph takes the family back home to Galilee.

The Matthew account of the early years of Christ is told from Joseph's perspective, including concerns about harsh realities of violent rulers. Yet Joseph relies on God's guidance, as must we.

Pleasing God First

'Your task is to single-mindedly serve Christ. Do that and you'll kill two birds with one stone: pleasing the God above you and proving your worth to the people around you' (Romans 14:18, MSG).

In a single verse (40) Luke covers Jesus' Nazareth childhood up to age twelve. Mary and Joseph know the joy of seeing their son growing and developing in mind and body. We don't have details, but we note Jesus' true humanity. His divine nature does not pre-empt it.

He knows the blessing of a good, godly home. Many of us can thank God for those who cared for us and those who formally or informally gave us our earliest inklings of God's truth and love.

Part of his parents' devotion to God is their conformity to the law of Moses. This includes the custom of every male adult appearing before the Lord at certain annual festivals (Exodus 23:17). In Jesus' day that means at the temple. We don't know if this is Jesus' first visit to the temple since his parents presented him there for infant dedication, but Luke records it as a significant visit. At age twelve, boys began to learn a trade and took Jewish instruction in preparation for becoming 'sons of the law'.

The crux of the visit comes when Jesus' parents discover he's not with the homeward-bound travellers. They return to Jerusalem and find him in the temple among the rabbis. Their relief turns to astonishment as they hear him both asking questions and giving answers (vv. 46, 47). In true rabbinical style, Jesus answers Mary's question about why he stayed behind with his own question: 'Did you not know that I was bound to be in my Father's house?' (v. 49, *NEB*).

In spite of Jesus' growing awareness of his mission, he returns home and deferentially continues under his parents' direction. Luke says that both God and people like what they see in the maturing Jesus (v. 52). If we mean to serve Jesus by living for him, we too will be pleasing to God. A by-product will sometimes be people's approval as well, but only if our goal is to please God first.

Deep Trust

'But I trust in your unfailing love' (v. 5).

This psalm and Commissioner Keith Banks's poem, 'Deep Trust', help us appropriately to close the year. Keith wrote the poem as he and his wife Pauline were about to retire from active Salvation Army officership.

> What can we say?
> For it would seem
> That God has worked
> Beyond our dream.
> Our prayers were made
> In simple trust;
> We said, 'Dear God,
> You simply must
> Attend our prayers,
> Work miracles.'
> Our faith was reaching pinnacles.
>
> But we must drop
> The selfish 'must',
> We centre solely
> On deep trust.
> We know you hold our destiny;
> Your love for us
> Bears scrutiny.
> So trust we did,
> And trust we still;
> We leave ourselves
> Within your will.
>
> What safer place
> Could ever be
> From now until
> Eternity?[30]

Notes

1, 2, 3. William Barclay, *The Daily Study Bible Series: The Letters to the Corinthians* (St Andrew Press, Edinburgh, 1954, revised and updated by St Andrew Press, 1975).

4. *Beacon Bible Commentary, vol.VIII* (Beacon Hill Press, Kansas City, MO, USA, 1968).

5. John Wesley, *Explanatory Notes upon the New Testament* (Epworth Press, London, 1958) (reprint).

6. *Christianity Today*, October 2006.

7. J. Oswald Sanders, *Spiritual Maturity* (Moody Press, Chicago, USA, 1962).

8. Deborah Douglas, *The Praying Life* (Morehouse Publishing, Harrisburg, PA, USA, 2003).

9. Normajean Honsberger, *Will You Choose Joy?: Reflections on Philippians* (Others Press, The Salvation Army, New York, USA, 2009).

10. Leslie Weatherhead, *A Private House of Prayer* (Hodder & Stoughton, 1958).

11. J. Sidlow Baxter, *Awake, My Heart* (Zondervan Publishing House, Grand Rapids, MI, USA, 1960).

12. Marva Dawn, *Being Well When We're Ill* (Augsburg Books, Minneapolis, MN, USA, 2008).

13. Tony Snow, 'Cancer's Unexpected Blessings', *Christianity Today*, July 2007, vol. 51, no. 7.

14. Andrew S. Miller, 'Suffering For and To Christ', a paper for the Wesleyan Theological Society Annual Meeting 2007.

15. Bramwell Booth, 'Conformed to Christ's Death', in *Our Master: Thoughts for Salvationists about their Lord* (Simpkin, Marshall, Hamilton, Kent & Co, Ltd, London, 1908).

16. *The Salvation Army's Declaration on Health, Healing and Wholeness* (written in Nagercoil, India, 1995).

17. *The Mission*, words and music by Jon Mohr and Randall Dennis. © 1989, Feed and Seed Music/J. R. Dennis Music.

18. *Companion to the Song Book of The Salvation Army*, compiled by Gordon Avery (Salvationist Publishing and Supplies, Ltd, London, 1961, 2nd edn 1962).

19. E. Stanley Jones, *Growing Spiritually* (Abingdon Press, New York, USA, 1953).

20. *Beacon Bible Commentary, vol. I* (Beacon Hill Press, Kansas City, MO, USA, 1969).

21. E. M. Bounds, *The Complete Works of E. M. Bounds* (Baker Book House, Grand Rapids, MI, USA, 1990).

22. John Wesley, *A Plain Account of Christian Perfection* (Beacon Hill Press, Kansas City, MO, USA, 1966, reprint).

23. William Barclay, *The Daily Study Bible Series: The Gospel of Luke* (St Andrew Press, Edinburgh, 1953, revised edn, 1975, published by Westminster Press, Philadelphia, PA, USA).

24. Jack Hayford, *The Mary Miracle* (Regal Books, Ventura, CA, USA, 1994).

25. 'Simeon's Song', music and words by Keith Banks, from *Sing a Song of Christmas* © The Salvation Army.

26. 'Chrismons' copyright held by Ascension Lutheran Church, Danville, VA, USA.

27. Flora Larsson, *Just a Year, Lord* (The Salvation Army, 2001; and originally in *God in My Everyday*, Hodder & Stoughton, 1984).

28. Luci Shaw, *Listen to the Green* (Harold Shaw Publishers, Wheaton, IL, USA, 1971).

29. William Barclay, *The Daily Study Bible Series: The Gospel of Matthew, vol. 2* (St Andrew Press, Edinburgh, 1953, revised and updated by St Andrew Press, 2001).

30. From the CD, *The Greatest Adventure* © The Salvation Army 2008.

Index

Subscribe...

Words of Life is published three times a year:
January–April, May–August and September–December

Four easy ways to subscribe
- By post – simply complete and return the subscription form below
- By phone – +44 (0)1933 445 445
- By email – mail_order@sp-s.co.uk
- Or visit your local Christian bookshop

SUBSCRIPTION FORM

Name (Miss, Mrs, Ms, Mr)...

Address ....

....

.... Postcode ....

Tel. No...

Email* ....

Annual Subscription Rates
UK £10.50   *Non-UK* £10.50 + £3.90 P&P = **£14.40**
Please send me .... copy/copies of the next three issues of *Words of Life* commencing with **January 2011**

Total: £ .... **I enclose payment by cheque** ☐
Please make cheques payable to *The Salvation Army*

Please debit my Access/Mastercard/Visa/American Express/Switch card

Card No. ☐☐☐☐ ☐☐☐☐ ☐☐☐☐ ☐☐☐☐   **Expiry date:** ___ /___

Security No. ☐☐☐ **Issue number (Switch only)** _____

Cardholder's signature: .... **Date:** ....

Please send this form and any cheques to: **The Mail Order Department, Salvationist Publishing and Supplies, 66–78 Denington Road, Denington Industrial Estate, Wellingborough, Northamptonshire NN8 2QH, UK**

☐ *We would like to keep in touch with you by placing you on our mailing list. If you would prefer not to receive correspondence from us, please tick this box. The Salvation Army does not sell or lease its mailing lists.